TABLE OF CONTENTS

YOU TOO CAN BE A
Fitness Model

CLARK BARTRAM

HATHERLEIGH PRESS · NEW YORK

You Too Can Be A Fitness Model
A Hatherleigh Press/Getfitnow.com Book

Hatherleigh Press/Getfitnow.com Books
An Affiliate of W.W. Norton and Company, Inc.
5-22 46th Avenue, Suite 200
Long Island City, NY 11101
Toll Free 1-800-528-2550
Visit our websites getfitnow.com and hatherleighpress.com

Library of Congress Cataloging-in-Publication Data

TO COME

Disclaimer:
Before beginning any exercise program, consult your physician. The author and the publisher disclaim any liability, personal or professional, resulting from the application or
misapplication of any of the information in this publication.

YOU TOO CAN BE A FITNESS MODEL books are available for bulk purchase, special pro-
motions and premiums. For more information on reselling and special purchase opportunities, please call us at 1-800-528-2550 and ask for the Special Sales Manager.

Cover Design by Fatema Tarzi
Interior Design by Angel Harleycat
Cover Photo by Jason Ellis
Additional Photos by Jason Ellis, Rick Schaff,
Anita Bartram, Julie Lykins and David Paul.

10 9 8 7 6 5 4 3 2 1
Printed in Canada.

PREFACE

By Rich King

Clark has been one of my best friends since the second grade. Although our lives have moved in paths that would seem very far removed in some ways, we have kept in contact all of our lives. Most people lose contact with their childhood friends, yet when Clark left Canton, Ohio for the Marine Corps when he was just seventeen, I somehow knew that our friendship would continue for life. While I was married at a young age and a father shortly after my nineteenth birthday, Clark was a United States Marine. Typical for Clark, he wasn't just any Marine, he was ranked second in his boot camp class.

As I worked hard to develop a career as a software engineer, Clark became more interested in physical fitness. He started working in a fitness center and became dedicated to weight training. His body's response to the weight training was phenomenal. He even entered a bodybuilding contest and won. I began to wonder when he was going to move back home and get a "real job." Again, typical Clark, he quickly became one of the youngest managers of one of the largest fitness center chains in the country. He continued bodybuilding and dedicated himself to managing the fitness center.

It was at this time that he started to get noticed more and more. He did a commercial for a shovel manufacturer and his picture appeared on the cover of a weightlifting glove package. I think it was at that point that he realized that he had what it took to make it as a fitness model. He began approaching photographers and friends that he met in the fitness industry to use him for photo shoots and ads. He even got himself an audition for *Kiana's Flex Appeal*. At that point I was still thinking, "Why doesn't this guy just move back home and manage a fitness center here where the cost of living is much less?" Again, typical Clark, he got the Kiana job. By this point in time, I was beginning to learn something new about my lifelong friend. He doesn't give up and he reaches his goals.

Since the Kiana gig, things have really been happening for Clark.

From his own fitness show, *American Health and Fitness*, to thirty or more magazine covers, he's been a commentator for bodybuilding contests for *ESPN* and has become a motivational speaker. There is no doubt that Clark is genetically gifted. However, in my opinion, that is not why he is where he is today. He is not the biggest guy in the gym. (Although I have no doubt that he could be if he wanted to be.) Instead, he has concentrated on perfect symmetry and unbelievable leanness. Look at him. Like I said, he meets his goals.

He also has an unbelievable knack for people. He's a great networker and he always has a plan. I've tried to nail down the key to Clark's success in one word and I've realized I can't. I think Clark's success has resulted in his being tenacious, driven, hard-working, personable, honest, he sincerely cares about people, but more importantly, he's humble. I know that seems hard to believe when you look at him, but he truly is. That's why he shows up on time, offers to help carry things, and doesn't snap when things don't go quite right. He's just Clark.

One parallel in our lives has been a passion for weight training. When he comes home to visit or when I visit him in California, one of the things we always make a point of doing is training together. I'm a software engineer in my late thirties, I need to lose thirty pounds, my legs are lagging behind my upper body and I don't have his looks. Yet when we are training together, it's like we're back in high school. When we are training, it doesn't feel like he's a fitness celebrity, has his own TV show and has been on over thirty magazine covers. He's just Clark, the guy I grew up with. If anyone can make your road to success a little less bumpy, it's Clark.

FOREWORD

By Ralph DeHaan

As a freelance photographer for the fitness industry, I have been photographing bodybuilders, fitness competitors and fitness models for the last fifteen years. I have shot for almost every fitness magazine on the market and have worked as a contract photographer for *Joe Weider* for part of that time. As you can imagine, I have been exposed to every kind of person in the industry.

Now that you know a little about me, I would like to tell you a little something about Clark Bartram. One day I was shopping in a local surf shop when an energetic young man approached me. He recognized who I was and began to explain that he was interested in breaking into the world of fitness modeling/bodybuilding. Keep in mind how many people I have worked with and how many times I have heard this same speech. I proceeded to give Clark my card and suggested that he call me when he felt he was ready to be photographed. His immediate response was, "I'm ready today!"

When I first looked at Clark, it was easy to see he had the raw elements to live his dream. He was extremely fit, good-looking and possessed more energy than I had seen in a while. What was yet to be seen was his consistency, follow through and strong desire to make it in this competitive industry.

As we went on our own ways, I suggested that Clark call me in a month or so because of my hectic traveling schedule with Weider. Exactly one month later I received a call from Clark, ready and willing to shoot. I regretted to inform him that my schedule was still as tight as ever and wasn't sure when we could take pictures. In my experience, this is when most people stop calling—not Clark. He stayed in touch and always reminded me he was in great shape and ready to photograph. I truly appreciated his persistence and enthusiasm because I always need new people to model. The problem is that I just don't have the time to keep up with people that I have chance encounters with.

Well, the time came when I had a small assignment to shoot a shoulder workout (it actually consisted of only one photo). And guess who I had just heard from a few days before? That's right—Clark! And I am sure you can guess who got the job.

I could go on and on about how Clark has followed through over the years even as his career has blossomed into one of the most successful I have seen in all my years as a fitness photographer. I have heard many people say that they have what it takes to be the next fitness superstar, but Clark is one of the only ones I have seen follow through with his plan.

Our relationship has grown over the years and so has the amount we work together. Clark has introduced me to several people whom I would have never met without him. He has gotten me work as a photographer with magazines simply because he has taken it upon himself to call and say that he wanted to be on their cover. He has assisted me on the other side of the camera carrying lights or loading film *while I shot other models*. I haven't seen him let up yet. He maintains the same approach that got him where he is today. He still calls me all the time saying, "Ralph, I'm in shape and ready and willing to shoot."

If you desire to make it in this industry, Clark is the guy to teach you. Read this book and put what you learn to work and who knows what might happen. Maybe someday I'll be telling you to, "tighten those abs, smile, and have fun," as I photograph you for the pages of a national fitness magazine.

When you feel you are ready, be sure to give me a call. I'm always looking for the next fitness supermodel. And it could be you.

Introduction—
So, You Want to Be a Fitness Model?

This book is a practical guide to taking realistic steps toward working consistently as a fitness model in the very competitive fitness magazine industry. Each chapter offers a professional, insider's view of individual steps that, when followed, will lead you on a direct path to realizing your ultimate goals in what can be a very rewarding industry.

Realize that you probably won't get rich, even at the highest levels of fitness modeling. But you may get a little famous—maybe very famous. And you will have some great times, experiencing a unique recognition that comes with being among the best of the best in a group of hard-working fitness-intensive men and women. Being a fitness model is, in many ways, it's own reward. In many ways, that may be enough. And there can be much more in the way of rewards, with both new and exciting opportunities and monetary gain.

You will find that some of the information in each of the chapters will overlap somewhat. That information overlap is by design to allow each chapter to stand at least partially alone—because I'm assuming you'll go straight to the chapters that interest you most, returning to them for tips and motivation as you work overtime to realize your goals. I'm assuming that because that's what I'll do.

The one challenge I offer you is to give this book one complete read-through from start to finish. If there are a thousand ways for every thousand people who *make it* in the entertainment business, this book is an honest account of how at least *I* have enjoyed a wonderful level of success as a fitness model. My hope is that it can serve as a guideline for your "way," your story of success-in-the-making.

What this book *isn't* is a guarantee that you'll break into an extremely competitive industry. But it's a good first step, and hope-

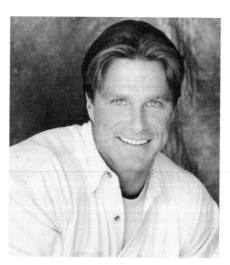

fully an outline for all the steps-to-success that follow.

The principles taught in this book apply to men and women alike. The common denominator in translating these principals into a reality—the realization of your ultimate professional fitness goals—is simply all about *effort.*

What finding success as a fitness model is *not* about is how good you look or how great your physique is. Those are necessary components in the equation, but not sufficient in what will ultimately lead to your success. No, success as a fitness model comes (like the cliché says) to whomever *wants it the most.* It is as simple as that.

I have seen many "shooting stars" in this industry blaze onto the scene almost as quickly as they faded away, only because they didn't put forth the effort to maintain a consistent level of success. It is too bad for them.

I have also seen scores of men and women who could easily grace the cover of any national fitness magazine if only given the chance or, more accurately, if they were equipped with the tools it takes to create their own opportunities in this highly competitive industry.

Many people over the years have asked me how I got where I am in the industry and, most importantly, how they can do the same. In the chapters to follow, you will read about the mental tools, strategies and proper attitude it takes to become a working fitness model in a competitive, but exciting, industry. With consistent effort and sacrifice, you can enjoy the rewards of being a well-known fitness model, turning your dreams into hard-fought realities.

Don't wait for your chance. *Make your dream a reality—and start today!*

Follow the Yellow Brick Road

Chapter 1—
Be Honest With Yourself: Do You Really Have What it Takes?

Editors, photographers, art directors and even their assistants are the people who will decide if you find yourself somewhere in the pages (or ideally on the cover) of a major fitness magazine. Editors, photographers, art directors and even their assistants are all very busy people.

A "normal" day for any one of these professionals involves having several deadlines to meet, fires to put out, locations to lock down, and models with attitudes to deal with. They have better things to do than deliberate over photos of people who think they can be the next Mike O'Hearn or Monica Brant, but really don't have a snowball's chance in a very warm place. So they *won't* deliberate over those photos and that doesn't make them bad people; it makes them people just like you, who have priorities and personal agendas and not a lot of time to waste.

What I'm trying to say is that now is the time to be honest about the "package" you present at this moment in your physical "evolution." Now is the time to stand before a mirror (or better yet, a Polaroid camera), and take a good look at yourself. And then, be honest—painfully honest. But also wonderfully honest (people that spend hundreds and thousands of hours working to sculpt their bodies sometimes get a little *too* critical, which does a disservice to what they may have to offer the world!).

Then informally pole three to five people whose opinion you know to be honest and realistic (which means parents and significant others may not be part of this list, as they may tend to be a little biased). Between these people and your own self-appraisal, try to answer the following questions: Do you have the caliber of physique that screams what it takes to be in the magazines or is your physique a little too close to the first photo in *"The New Theory of Evolution"* ad?

The New Theory of Evolution

(Unretouched photos taken over a period of less than 12 weeks.)

Brought to You By

⊙EAS
EXPERIMENTAL AND APPLIED SCIENCES

The World's Leading Supplier of
Sports Nutritional Supplements
for the Evolving Man

www.eas.com

We're not talking about just a nice body, but a superior degree of symmetry that is pleasing to the eye—and camera lens. There has to be a balance between all your body parts, because the people that will hire you don't have the time or money to hide major physical imbalances. The whole point of their publication is to use your photographic image to help sell a lifestyle of exercise, nutrition and mental balance!

You don't have to be (and may not want to be) physically huge, depending on the style of fitness magazine you're targeting. But do you have awesome muscle tone, the kind that would catch your own eye and make you want to spend your hard-earned dollars on a magazine or fitness product purchase? Rate your muscular definition—and be sure to focus on the classic trouble areas (usually the abs for men, the hips and thighs for women) and not just your favorite body parts.

Now, do you have the face to match the great physique? And is your face a face that "the camera likes?" Ask someone who's taken photographs to shoot informal test photos of you in a natural light environment (early morning or late afternoon), and then rate the way your facial features "play" to the camera. This is also a great way to learn how you can best "play" to the camera and which camera angles favor your facial features—without the pressure of a professional shoot!

A semi-professional, casual photo shoot gives you a fair chance to rate how your features "read" in front of a camera. In every group of working models, there's invariably someone who grew up as a "plain Jane" or "plain Jim," someone whose features come to life in the "magic world" of film! You hear about it all the time—the model who says they didn't realize how beautiful they were until people started asking them to pose. You may just have the face that makes you a "sleeper" professional model—but you'll only find out if you take a little, informal chance!

Remember, being honest with yourself means developing your own "critical eye." (And the process should be fun, too. How many photos in fitness magazines do you see where the fitness models *don't* look like they're having fun?)

You'll become your own best critic, as you cut through the layers of self-doubt or over-expectations (and often both) and treat your course as a fitness model with an objectivity that will empower you to identify and improve on the tangible results of all your hard work!

Ultimately, I'm trying to save you needless embarrassment, or the hassle of wasting your time. Trust me, the previously mentioned magazine professionals will be painfully more honest than I have been. (And take heart; if you don't have "it" now, it doesn't mean you won't have "it" a year from now, in a couple years, or even after a decade of hard work!)

So let's say you have what it takes. What's next? That's the question that you have asked yourself, as so many other fledgling fitness models have asked themselves too. You may have even asked yourself "The Big Question" that got you to pick up this book: "If Clark Bartram can do it, why can't I?" I agree.

If I can do it then why not you? So we move onto the next chapter—and the next step—how you, too, can grace the covers of some national fitness magazines, or at least carve out your own space on the pages inside!

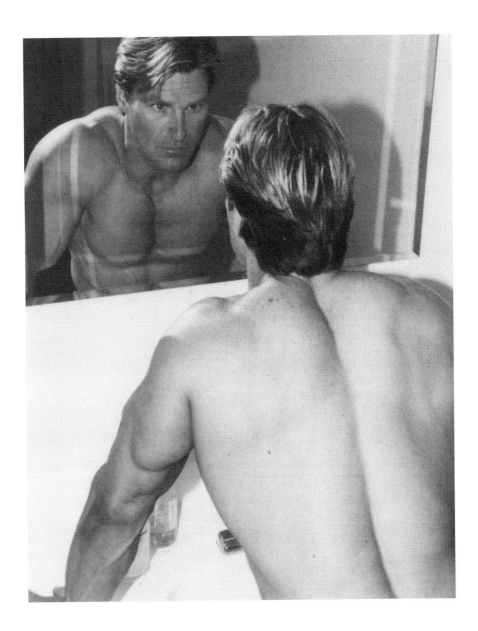

Chapter 2—
Put Your Best Foot Forward!

Okay, you have the look that will make America (and maybe even the rest of the world) pick up your issue. How do you get there? How do you find your way through the maze of competition and natural obstacles to becoming a working fitness model? How do you even *find the maze?* How in the world do you (and all your hard work in the gym) finally get noticed?

Well, I have the answer and I'm going to tell you not only how I got where I am, but also what I do to stay on top of my game. So now, you may ask yourself, "Why would Clark do this. Why would he nurture the competition?"

Well, of course, to sell my book. Let's not be naive. But also, the one thing that I have learned in this business and in my lifetime is that it is better to give someone a hand up than it is to try and keep someone down. Being a "nice guy" or "nice girl" in this industry doesn't necessarily mean you're going to finish last. The hard-working editors, art directors and photographers (with their pick of the world's pretty, in-shape people) are just like anybody else—they *want* to spend their long, hard days working with nice people. So it's good business.

I also realize that there is much undiscovered talent—and I'm certainly not the only one who has what it takes. Bringing up undiscovered talent means you may have somebody in your corner in years to come who might be able to return the favor. So, again, it's good business.

But ultimately, after you've had some success and feel like you're on top of the world, and then later realize your rent and phone bill still have to be paid, you quickly come to realize that how you tackle this business, or any business, isn't too far from how you should lead your life. Helping other people is, at the end of the day, just a nicer way to live your life.

I have noticed time and again that the old cliché, "what goes

around, comes around," is a proven cliché for a reason. Good luck does come to good people! Good people (in a position to hire you) tend to hire other good people, too!

So now you need to get the attention of the right people. We will discuss in later chapters just *who* those people are, and *how* you get them to see you. But first things first: get in shape! Yes, I said, *"Get in shape!"*

You might think you look good right now, but remember: there are *so* many people reaching and sweating for the same goal that you are. You have to be better than the next guy or girl.

So, take a few weeks and dedicate that time to training hard, getting a healthy tan, the obligatory body-shave and, as important as all the above, some beauty sleep.

Nothing is as difficult to fake in front of the camera as the natural "glow" that comes with being well rested. Nothing is as hard to hide as being burned-out when the whole point of you being in front of the camera is to sell clean, fresh, robust health!

We are going to do a photo shoot. And guess what? I'm going to get you ready, the way *I* get ready.

Now don't run off and hire a first class photographer, lighting specialist and airbrush artist. The people that will hire you only want to see some candid snapshots or even a Polaroid will do. Again, the only thing you'll need to do is be in shape—really good shape.

I can't stress this enough. You know the old saying: "You only have one chance to make a first impression." Trust me on this one. You *will* only have one chance. Remember that these are busy people who have thousands of wannabes saying, "Look at me!"

Don't blow it. And be prepared to have fun—or else!

Chapter 3—
Your Photo Shoot.

Once you get the opinion of three to five trustworthy, non-biased people who have all given you a thumbs up that the "package" you're presenting is ready to unveil, it's time to shoot!

Get your Polaroid or 35mm camera (it can be automatic) and snap a roll of 24 or 36 prints. Stand against a white wall with nothing on it. You'll want to use a little lighting here to help mold and highlight your facial features and physique. Try positioning yourself so that a dominant lamp (or better yet, the sun) hits you at a three-quarter to side angle to the direction you're facing. Then on the other side of your face, use a "fill" source or "bounce board" (like a big piece of white poster board) three-quarter to directly under the camera's lower frame.

Shoot your first roll. This is a test shoot, experimenting with light and camera placement. Find out what makes you look best.

Oh yeah, I almost forgot. What should you wear? There is no need to run off and buy a new wardrobe—unless of course, you don't own any shorts.

Make sure your shorts aren't too tight around the waist or fit too snug on the legs around the mid-thigh or higher. Solid colors are best—definitely no patterns or stripes.

Showing off your abs and overall midsection is of utmost importance. I'll tell you later how to dial them in to perfection. Consider your abs your entrance pass to the party, and get them as tight as you can (especially with diet) before you shoot your preliminary photos.

The photo that you will submit should be taken from the knees up. And for goodness sake—smile! Try not to be overtly sexy, as you're liable to look just downright silly. Trust me on this: magazine professionals hate that stuff unless they ask you to do it.

They also need to see if you have any teeth, which means being free with a natural smile that brightens up your face, starting with "those pearly whites." There are many people who have the body but not the face or smile to match. Fitness magazines are looking for the total package.

If you develop your photos and you don't like them, don't send them anywhere. Once again, get some unbiased help (three to five reliable people) to choose that winning shot.

So, now we have the shot that you (and your reliable, trusted, opinion-givers) love. What's next? Read on, my fitness friend.

Chapter 4—
The Photo is in the Mail.

So now it is time to make the "Money Move."

Later in this book, I will provide you with the names, phone numbers and addresses of the "right people" who can get you working as a fitness model.

I will also provide you with the information of top national photographers, and I'll provide you with the most up-to-date information on contacts at most of the major fitness and bodybuilding magazines in the industry. And we'll also take a look at the overseas market and supplement manufacturers. But first, let's look at what you need to send them.

The first thing you will want to do is write a cover letter. Introduce yourself and give the people you are trying to work with basic personal information about yourself, and about your love for the lifestyle and the gym. Most importantly, express how you are interested in modeling for them, in *filling their needs* as a representative for their publication. (Your picture is being used to "sell" the ideas and principles that define their magazine, so you bet you're a representative for them!)

Don't be too wordy—be straight and to the point. (It's not a bad idea to have a friend who works with business-style writing or even a business secretary look the letter over.)

On a separate sheet of paper, type the following information:

- Height
- Weight
- Hair Color
- Eye Color
- Body Fat Percentage

Women will want to include their measurements. You'll notice I omitted age. Your age is really your business. For some producers, there is a chance your age may work against you. What you're selling is your physique, your "look," and your personality. Age won't be relevant if you do your job and sell those three things.

In addition to this information, include all contact information such as your name, mailing address (women especially might want to use a PO box number), e-mail address, and the best time for someone to contact you.

Don't be sloppy! Type the cover letter and vital statistics letter or have someone who types well format and type it for you. Try to use a computer with spell check. Your data will be placed in a file and you will be remembered by this information, so put a little effort into it and make it as perfect as you can!

Above all, in your cover letter—your extension of the package you present—don't sound desperate! This won't help at all! Desperation is tacky and makes people uncomfortable. Uncomfortable people will tend not to hire you. You may feel very desperate inside, but you must ignore that desperation—or hide it. I suggest you face it and try to overcome it.

What works for me is to try to identify if I'm hoping to get this particular job a little too much, and if I'm letting my real motivation shine through in my cover letter, in the actual audition (especially), and in my follow-ups. And if I am, I ask myself, "Why?" Do I need to make the rent? Is Christmas coming? Am I not feeling as good about myself as did when I had peaked two months ago, and nailing an audition would make me feel better?

None of these reasons for being desperate—no matter how valid and true they may be—will help get you the job. I find that the best non-desperate way to motivate myself to get a job is to forget or try to let go of that negative motivation. I remind myself what I love about being in the best shape that I can be, what a privilege it is being blessed with good bone structure and a personality that I can communicate to the camera, and about how fun the work is.

So with your head in the right place, stick to the facts and don't embellish or oversell yourself. Trust me. The people who will hire

SAMPLE COVER LETTER

Dear Mr. Dixon:

Please allow me to take a few minutes out of your busy schedule to introduce myself.

My name is Clark Bartram and I am very interested in modeling for Men's Health magazine.
Enclosed are current photos taken of me in the format that seems to be working so successfully for your publication. An exact set has already been sent to Mr. Karabotsos.

I have a goal to someday grace the cover of your magazine and hopefully these photos will convince you that I have what it takes. Please feel free to contact me when you have had a chance to review the pictures.

I will contact you regarding my potential involvement in one week if I haven't already heard back from someone. I thank you for your time and consideration and I hope I have a chance to achieve this goal.

Have a healthy day,

Clark W. Bartram
(phone number) home
(phone number) cell

SAMPLE RESUME

CLARK BARTRAM

TELEVISION
American Health & Fitness (Sandstone Pictures)	Host	Health Network
Shipshape Media Productions)	Host	AFN (Naval
Kiana's Flex Appeal (Entertainment)	Co-Host	ESPN2 (Wave
Fox 6 News	Fitness Correspondent	

INFOMMERCIALS
List available upon request

COMMERCIALS
List available upon request

PRINT
Muscle & Fitness	2 Covers	(Photographers Corey Sorenson & Kal Yee)
Physical	Cover	
Gym	Cover	(Photographer Ralph DeHaan)
Natural Bodybuilding	2 Covers	(Photographer Ralph DeHaan)

TRAINING
Actor's Workshop-Commercial John Hammil	Ongoing
Teleprompter Nick Kellis	Ongoing
Voice Over Nick Kellis	Ongoing

SPECIAL SKILLS
Extensive Public Speaking
Television Commentary
Voice Overs
Perform Strength Feats
Excellent in all sports

SAMPLE STATS SHEET

Clark Bartram

Height	5'9" / 5'10"
Weight	185-190 lbs.
Measurements	30" waist, 32" inseam
Body Fat Percentage	7-8% year-round
Shoe Size	10.5
Jacket	44 regular
Eye Color	Blue
Hair Color	Dark blonde/brown

you only care how you look. They don't care what you say—unless you say things that make them not want to hire you! Enough said. If you decide to tackle your introduction to the hiring people in another way, I ask that you don't come crying to me. Try not to cry at all; the point of this process is that it should be fun!

Now, you have your photo, cover letter, and stats sheet. Time to package up your future! Now take a moment and consider this from the "receiving end." If *you* were getting a ton of mail everyday, which letters and correspondence would you give your immediate attention? The ones that looked the most important!

With this in mind, spend a few extra dollars and use *Fed Ex*. It is more expensive, but I've found it will be well worth the $18 it costs for you to be on the top of the list in the mind of the right person. It is the *Gucci* of professional correspondence worldwide. Business people respect it—and will respect you.

Now we play the waiting game.

Chapter 5—
Put Your Ego Aside.

Yeah, we already know you look better than those other fitness models and you deserve to be there instead of them. You know it because you believe in your potential; I know it because you've read this far.

Now the dose of reality: don't expect your phone to be ringing off the hook. It won't. On these pages, I'm going to give it to you straight. If you can't handle it, that's unfortunate because it's only going to get more painful for you as progress with each step in the process. I'm playing devil's advocate here.

Conversely, just because your phone didn't ring right away also doesn't mean it's a done deal. You don't hear the fat lady singing, do you? Hopefully the fat lady isn't you!

Once you get into shape, you absolutely had better stay that way. And if and when you do get a call you better be ready to shoot tomorrow. That's how quickly it works. That is how I built my career. I made a statement early on by letting everyone know that I am always ready to shoot—by always being in "shoot-able" shape.

The last, very last, and *absolutely* last thing the magazine professionals want to hear is, "Give me six weeks and I'll be ready." There have been several times when I wasn't the first choice, but I got the job because the first choice wasn't ready, or available. I don't care how I get the job, I only care that I get it. And the old saying, "luck is simply the meeting of opportunity and preparation," couldn't be truer than in this example.

It could be months before you get a call. It could even be a year, but I suggest you don't give up. If you've read this far, worked this hard, and truly believe you have what it takes, then don't quit.

And remember that I'm not guaranteeing you any work. I'm only guaranteeing that you now have some powerful tools to take the right steps on how to get noticed. We're going to continue learning that process, and then the rest—*the action*—is up to you. And the actions you take, with persistence, sacrifice and a little luck may be just what *they* are looking for!

Chapter 6—
Follow-Up.

Always remember that magazine editors, art directors and photographers are all busy people with *so much* more on their mind than, frankly, *you.*

Now the good news: remember they need new faces *all of the time.* Always remember this. You are excited, you're waiting for them to call and it's at the front of your mind at all times. Once again (I'll be redundant out of professional courtesy to the people I've worked with for a long time), these are busy people and unfortunately you cannot be the first thing on their minds. This doesn't mean they are not interested, only busy. So, now your job is to get them—and keep them—interested.

The squeaky wheel gets the grease. This old saying couldn't be truer. Write a follow-up letter. Make phone calls on a frequent basis. Only you can decide how often you follow-up. This is very subjective. I suggest you base your level of tenacity on the type of response you are getting from each individual contact at each individual magazine.

If someone says you're "fat and ugly," just don't call back. It's a tough business. I'm not the sharpest knife in the drawer, but even I would know how to take a response like that.

If someone says you're not right for what they have coming up, consider this person a professional who's being honest and considerate—and also someone who might remember you in a year or two, after you've made a little improvement. You will get varied responses.

Keep a log with dates of when you called, whom you talked to and what was said. Remember people change jobs, get fired, laid-off or whatever. "No" today might be, "Oh yeah, I've seen your photo," a year from now. Know the next person, and update your occasional follow-up correspondence and calls to know when there is a "next" person. Just because Jane didn't like you doesn't mean the next person won't. Also, Jane most likely left without telling her replacement that you will be calling. Get my drift?

So be courteous, be gracious and be smart. Be friendly and considerate. Do not be dumb. This isn't about your ego; it's about you getting work, and swallowing your ego for the good of your dream.

Above all, remember that you are not God's gift to *Joe Weider*. Arnold was.

(from left) Krista, Kathy, Clark, Tia, Melissa. Second season cast.

Chapter 7—
Who Needs an Agent?

I've got to be honest—honest at the risk of sounding cocky. I have yet to find someone who can match my excitement, passion and desire to help me succeed.

Let me back this up with a thumbnail statistic. I can count on one hand how many jobs I have gotten through an agency over the last decade. Agencies have their place; they can get people in to see the "big guns." But they also have their own agenda—to do everything they can to have one of their clients win the job, to get their percentage (usually 10 to 25 percent, sometimes out of your rate and sometimes over and above your day rate, depending on the job and magazine). They will call you and twenty other guys or girls.

Also, agencies tend not to be very proactive with regards to seeking out work. That means you will get a call to go to an interview/audition only when *they* get a call. The nice thing about the tips we're covering here (and if you follow the course outlined in this information) is that you will be way ahead of your competition—*even* the agencies.

Some agency fees are charged over and above your day rate, and magazines don't want to pay an agency fee any more than you do. Take advantage of that. I'm talking about beating down some doors here, but not to force your product (yourself) on anyone. To barge through the door as *the very solution the magazine is looking for!* Are you with me? Then let's do it.

You're going to need to save a little capital to send a strong message to the industry that you're about to crack into. Send out as many packages as you financially can afford. Get them out to everyone listed in this book. Allow a reasonable period of time for the packages to arrive and then, within about seven to ten days (so you don't appear too desperate), follow up and be consistent.

What will eventually happen is that you will get noticed—if you and the people you trust have been honest with you about whether you've got the goods. Remember, they need new faces, you just might be the face they've been looking for to launch the cover of their magazine.

To step back a little in the other direction, I will also provide you with a few names and numbers of agencies that specialize in fitness models if you want to hedge your bets and maximize your potential. It can't hurt.

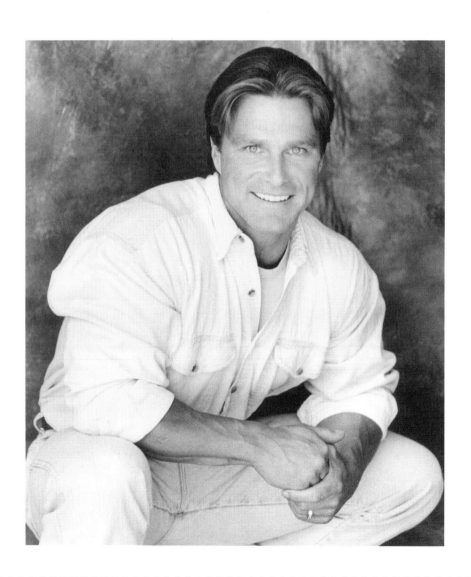

Chapter 8—
If at First You Don't Succeed, Try Again.

Okay, let's say six months has passed and you still haven't received that coveted "You're the very thing we're looking for," phone call. So now what?

Time to repeat the process all over again. There is a certain freedom in simply going back to step one of this book and tackling the routine from the best place to start—the very beginning.

You follow a routine all the time—every time you walk through the doors to your gym to fire up your workout. You've probably experienced and enjoyed that enormous satisfaction, or even a calming effect, that comes with overcoming each little challenge that makes up your workout routine. If you're training smart, you're modifying exercises, sets and reps along the way, but the familiarity of performing what really amounts to an invaluable ritual provides the powerful psychological boost that makes going to the gym such an important factor in your life.

The same approach applies to the steps we're working with here. Familiarize yourself with this ritual of success in the same way that you are so familiar with the ritual of success you perform every time you go to the gym!

So, it is back to the ritual that will lead to you becoming a working fitness model. Remember that editorial, art and photography staffs may very well have changed in the last six or so months. Your "type" may just be *the type* they're looking for, the hot look that will put you on the cutting edge. They might be looking for your type now, or they might not be. Whatever the case may be, just repeat the process again. And be prepared to do it again another six months down the road! But only if you want to succeed, of course.

How bad do you want it? I've been in this game for a long time. Do I still play "the games?" Do I still restart the process—my own ritual to success? You know the answer.

Keep it up until you are where you know you should be. And when you get there, don't stop. I haven't. So *that's* how Clark does it! Just think, maybe someday you'll get the nod over me. After all, I am getting older—but I am not getting any closer to giving up, either.

The beauty of our community is that we understand a little something about the rewards that come with goal setting, persistence and following through. Make those habits serve all aspects of your life. We're all in this because we love a challenge. So bring it on! I encourage you!

Whatever it takes to get the shot!

Chapter 9—
Location, Location, Location.

Here's the first, second and third law of real estate. If you are geographically challenged (meaning not in Southern California), chances are you'll have to be willing to conveniently be on vacation in California and extremely lucky with very fortuitous timing to walk into an art director's office and "land" a cover. Otherwise, your "vacation" will have to be of a more permanent—or at least consistent—variety if you want the job.

Now please, don't pack up and move to Venice Beach and start training at Gold's Gym. Heaven knows that too many people have already made that mistake (although it is a lovely and interesting town). Don't be the next fool who thinks, "If I only lived there, they'd be offering me contracts at the juice bar."

So location can become an issue, but there are ways around being in your *own* right place (let's say, Ohio) and still being available when the right time comes.

Once the decision-makers know who you are, you need to let them know how hard you're willing to work to make the process *easy for them*—not for you. Their job is hard enough already, being responsible for simply getting everything to the point where you can stand in front of the camera, and for everything that follows the shoot to get your magazine cover out on the stands.

Let editors, art directors and photographers know (early and often) that you are willing to fly wherever they need you. Most likely where they need you will be in Los Angeles. And most likely, they won't pay for your trip—unless you are the new "It" guy or girl, the next hot ticket on the scene.

I have friends that have been flown out from Florida—you could be next. Just don't bank on that possibility as you work hard to get noticed and make your mark "on the scene."

What I'm saying is that if you want it bad enough, you might have to foot your own bill for a non-paying or, at best, $500 (or most likely $300) gig. Like I told you earlier, you will not get rich as a fitness model—but you may get a little famous, opening doors that may not seem apparent right now.

Chapter 10—
Finally, Everyone Else Realizes What You Knew All Along.

So, you get the phone call: "We'd like you to come in for a session on such and such date with such and such photographer for such and such feature story" or (the Holy Grail)—a cover photo! Thank them, and then get ready! Now it's time for some tricks of the trade on how to look your best on that big day.

First of all, *be in shape*! All the tricks of the trade can't compare to being in shape. And all the tricks of the trade won't help either —unless your *tricks* are sacrifice and discipline, proper diet and years and years of smart, intense physical conditioning!

Be tanned. I have found that the best self-tanning product is *Jan Tana Fast Tan*. I shoot enough and have to be tanned so often that I've chosen to stay out of the sun and tanning beds to save my skin for future shoots. You make your own choice. If the UV-saving tan is a direction you want to go, you can call 1-800-Jantana and order their excellent *Fast Tan* product there. Ask for the application video and all the other necessary products as well. Of course, use as recommended.

Everybody who takes training in the gym seriously knows a little something about how elusive it is to "peak out" at the moment— or even the hour—that you need to be your physical best. *Nail it* and you feel empowered with the perfect combination of muscle tone and muscle definition. This confidence will show up dramatically in your personality and in the way the camera sees you.

I personally like to sodium deplete two days out from a shoot, *to dial myself in*. It's a bit complicated to explain in this book. I've been utilizing this process—under the pressure of a shoot or a contest—for several years, so I know what my body responds to best.

A common-sense tip when you're just starting out is to simply

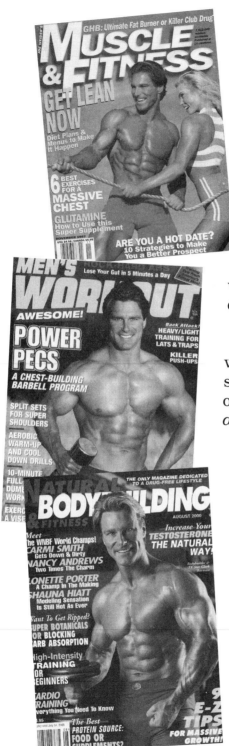

start setting "phantom" or rehearsal dates every six to ten weeks. Discipline yourself to try to "peak out" on the target date, even at a target time of day (most exterior photo shoots are in the morning before 10:00 a.m., or the late afternoon, starting three hours before sundown). Make it game for yourself, and take excellent notes of everything you try, every result you see and feel.

Hit your target "phantom date" with the passion of a real peak date—*but without the pressure!*

Also, read the magazines to see what diet/training processes and strategies other people use to "peak out." Above all, *talk to your doctor about which processes are safe* or may be a little too cutting edge for you.

Chapter 11—
Dialed in & Goin' Downtown! (The Day of Your Shoot.)

You've landed your first fitness model job. The best advice, again (is this sounding familiar?)—*be ready!*

Here the old cliché "you can't be prepared enough" is so true (actually you can, but best to over-prepare for your first couple of jobs—as long as you get plenty of sleep the night before!). I heard a quote I liked that went something like this: "Complete preparation is just proof before action that you've *already* done your job!"

Show up on time (or even a little early—about fifteen minutes early is perfect). Show up tanned and ripped, with new white shoes and plenty of bright clothing changes. Have in your bag some baby oil, gel and a towel (you're building a modeling "kit" here). And most of all, *bring a great attitude.*

And did I mention to SHOW UP ON TIME! Prompt fitness models are people that have a higher percentage of booking more work down the line!

There is nothing worse than a model with an attitude—especially one who is on his or her first big job, because that may very well be that model's *last* big job. I don't care how many local jobs you've nailed in your sleepy little (or big) town—you're in the big leagues now. Or at least you'd like to think so. So check your ego at the door (an under pressure hint: think about instances in advance where the people around you commented on your great attitude and try to replicate the mindset you had in those situations).

Be willing to carry boxes or assist with anything you see needs help. Don't be a brown noser or follow the camera guy around like a puppy, either. Just ask if there is any way you can help. Chances are, they will tell you "no," but you will leave a good impression for the next time.

I can't tell you how many times I've had production people tell me how impressed they were with a particular fitness model, a guy or girl who seemed like "one of the team." Those are the people that will speak up in a production meeting and say, "I'd like to work with him/her again. He/She's cool!" Sometimes that's all it takes to get you re-hired!

Photo shoots tend to either take all day or one hour. I used to have no idea why this was so. It just seemed to always work out to be all day when I had to be somewhere, and one hour when I had all day. (A hint: try *not to have to be somewhere.* And NEVER show up and hint that you hope it goes fast, because you have something more important to go do. They'll very likely have someone else more important to hire next time!)

Over time, I've come to realize that the duration of a photo shoot depends on what they need, who the photographer is and how you look. So if you are there all day, have a great attitude *all day.* Bring your cell phone or homework and be patient. Just jump up when they say they're ready for you. *Never make anyone wait on you!* (Be prepared to say, "Bye mom, call you later," and put the cell phone in the bag with the ringer off!).

You wait—not them!

Whatever ideas you have for how to present yourself when the camera starts clicking, store them in the back of your mind and save them. Then listen. If you're doing your job and *listening,* really in a "groove" with the photographer and everyone in front of and behind the camera, you'll have fun. You'll help create a lot of good shots. You'll find you'll smoothly nail what they want.

You're not being paid to work hard (even though you will work very hard). You're being paid to *remain relaxed and have fun, while under pressure,* and to share that sense of fun with the camera and the people who will buy the magazine that your image represents. There are worse ways to earn an honest wage.

If the shoot takes only one hour, don't be bummed. Sometimes that's all it takes. You've just beaten the curve, so feel good about yourself and go grab some food. Don't linger behind. And don't seem anxious.

Say your good-byes *clean:* "That was really fun. Do you have my headshot and/or composite card?" (Bring an extra three or five of each, just in case.) Maybe even say, "I hope we can all work together again sometime" at the most! THEY will most likely respond, "You did great, you have a great...." They usually want you to feel good, but they also want to pack up and get back to the office or go home.

If they liked you and you showed up with a great attitude and you were in fabulous shape, you will get called again. You will. You have just started to get into the loop. Again, it should seem obvious but everybody wants people like them—sometimes a little too much. *Make them love you by being yourself.* That is, if you are nice and have a good attitude. If you're not very nice (it happens), just be quiet and do what you're told. Oh, I almost forgot—wear deodorant and bring breath mints! You might have to shoot with another model. And they may have forgotten their deodorant and breath mints!

Be sure to read the section ***Lessons from the Other Side*** later in the book. It showcases a wealth of information from photographers, magazine and supplement company owners, make-up artists, stylists, and television producers.

Chapter 12—
How Do You Become the Next Fitness Superstar?

Good question. I guess I have to continually refer back to the beginning. Do you really have what it takes? If so, then here is what you need to do.

Evaluate anything you've done that has been effective and has lead to *success.*

Identify whatever hasn't worked—things you *got around* by good luck or good instincts. Prune the tree of the things that have held you back and continue to do everything that has worked to get you where you are today. Why try to reinvent the wheel? It worked so far, so why change? Maybe the "wheels" will keep the momentum going!

Stay in shape *all year round* and let everyone know that is what you are doing. The people who can hire you will come to think of you as an immediate solution to the thousand unforeseeable circumstances that make their days very crazy at times.

You have made some good connections and developed relationships with the right contacts, at least to some degree (if you were smart). Now it's time to take it to the next level. Call these people back.

Let's say the contact you wish to maintain your working relationship with is a photographer. Call him or her once a month and remind them that you're out there and ready to shoot. *Do not become a pest.*

Be sensitive and considerate and remember that they are very busy people. You are not the only thing on their mind, so it is up to you to not only remind them you are out there, but that you are out there as a *potential solution* to whatever problem falls on their plate.

It's as easy as dialing their voice mail to say, "Hey, Chuck, hope your apparel shoot went great. Just wanted to let you know I'm available and training hard and looking pretty lean. Thanks for keeping me in mind for anything you have coming up. I'll keep in touch." Do this with everyone you meet.

Finally, after your shoot, immediately write a thank-you letter to your contact person—the person who hired you. Let them know how grateful you are for the opportunity and you'll be ready to work with them wherever and whenever they need you.

Chapter 13—
Become a Master of Self-Promotion.

Remember that no one has ever believed in me as much as I have believed in myself (my Mom excluded, of course). During the shoot, check your ego at the door as you become your own ad agency, agent, manager, publicist, PR representative and cheerleader.

This is a delicate balance that deserves some discussion. If you are not very careful, you can come out looking very self-centered and blatantly stuck up. People tend to not want to hire an annoying ego. Your look may be hot now, but if you're really annoying, they'll just work that much harder to find someone with a similar hot look—*sans the attitude!*

But if you play things correctly, you will be your own best representative. Build and keep a database of all of the contacts you are making. Send non-specific holiday cards. For example, just because you celebrate Christmas doesn't mean they do. Send a Happy Holidays card instead. You have already sent your thank-you note, so be careful and selective to avoid looking too anxious or fake.

The bottom line here is to keep your name fresh and out there. Don't ever think you will be remembered because of your cute dimples (high or low). Always be considering some reason to get them thinking of you. And give them that reason with taste, tact and class. You are your product and want to always be on top of your game—physically and mentally.

Cultivate these new relationships and make the most of each one. I'll say it again: you are your product. Part of your job now is to always sell yourself.

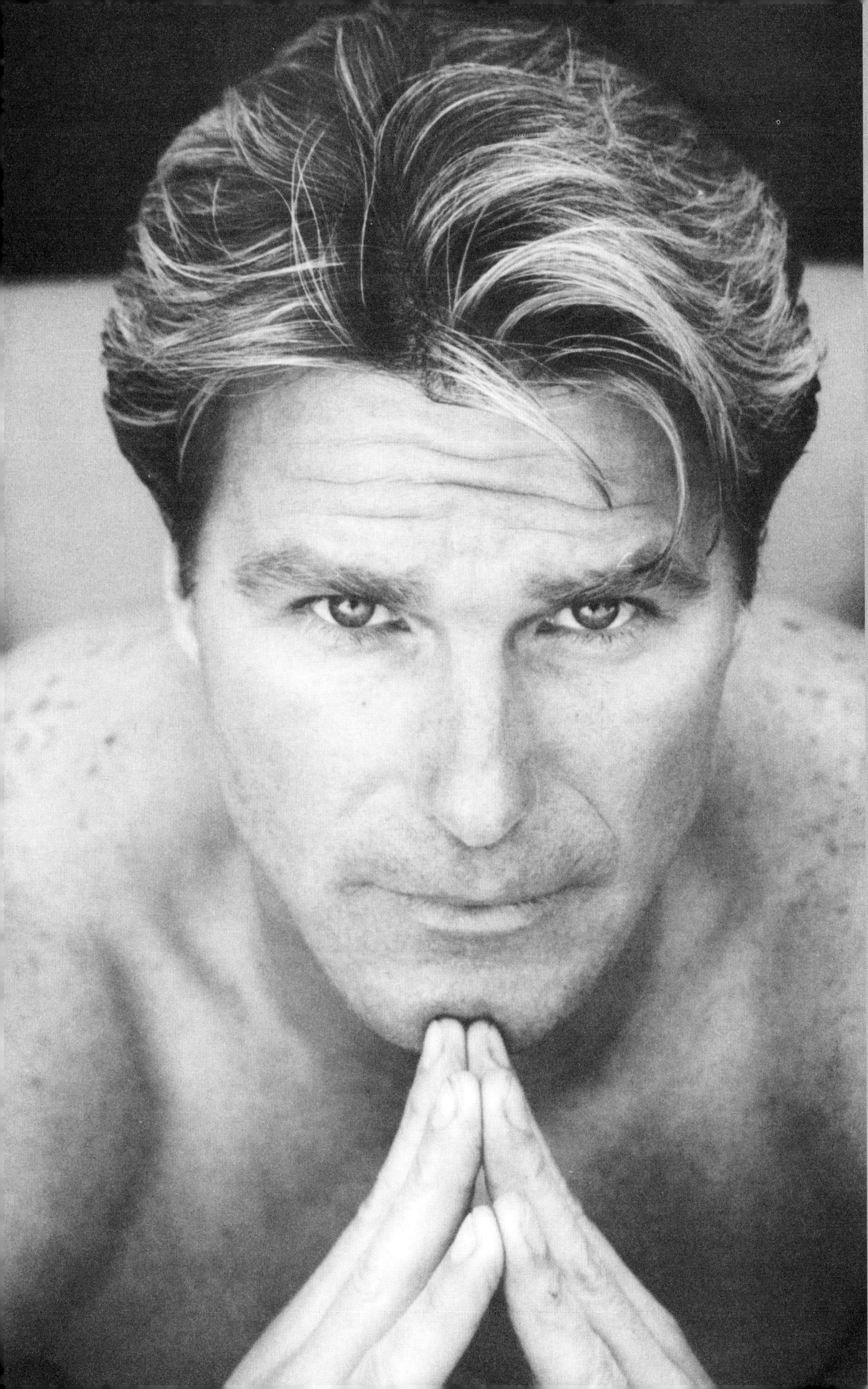

YOU TOO CAN BE A Fitness Model

Chapter 14—
Help Others Get Where You Are.

I have helped a lot of people get in magazines and on television. I've utilized whatever connections I had available to me for these people. So why did I perform (and continue to perform) this puzzling act of unselfishness?

Perhaps because the only thing more unattractive than the person who lacks confidence is the person who thinks he or she is the only one deserving of success!

You'll notice I'm omitting why being "a giver" is just a plain old nice thing to do or why Mom or Dad would be more proud of you for doing it. We're talking about *good business* here. *Nice actions get talked about and remembered by people that hire you or can help you get hired.*

So help someone out. Don't be a jerk. Obviously, if you're a man, it's easier and more self-serving to help out women fitness models because they can work *with you.* But I have offered my help to guys who could very likely beat me out for the job, as well as for jobs down the road. Most people want that kind of help.

Don't use this as some cheap pick up line for the attractive person on the stair climber. If you see someone training hard in the gym and you think they have what it takes, let them know. Don't make any promises. Just let them know that there is a chance you can get their information to the right people.

This will only be a positive reflection on you. Offering potential colleagues and potential competitors advice and a "leg up" will make you look good on both ends of the deal—for the simple price of a phone call or two. Plus, you're creating another opportunity for the "powers that be" to be reminded of you.

At the very least, you're generating energy by talking about something that you've worked hard to excel at. An earnest conversation about shared achievements will make you feel empowered! It feels good to help someone else out. Don't be selfish. And if you are, I hope for your sake that you're not attracting people to control your career who are also selfish, but you probably are.

The Bible says that you reap what you sew. Sew some good for someone else—and you'll most likely sew a little good fortune for yourself at the same time!

Clark, Jack Lalanne, and Steve during the taping of "Shipshape."

Chapter 15—
Be Modest.

If you happen to begin your fifteen minutes of fame, here's the best piece of advice I can ever offer—put effort—*real* effort—into not getting a big head.

This is a moment to moment temptation that will be hard at times to keep in check. To push yourself to look as good as a working fitness cover model breeds a certain cockiness. However, it also breeds good, old-fashioned discipline.

Now it's time to exercise that discipline. You'll have it all in perspective and then, voila! There's that hot guy/girl at the gym who has never even made eye contact with you and now he/she's driving the row of ab crunchers to a grinding halt, making his/her way over to *you!* Okay, that part is fun.

And in a month the next new magazine will be out featuring someone who's a little more cut, lit a little better, and tanned a little more golden *than you*. There is nothing uglier than someone with a conceited attitude. Especially because that self-inflicted disease leaves you feeling empty—because it's not real!

Imagine that nice girl (or guy) in the gym, the one you've always admired because she had the "stuff," carrying herself with confidence, yet modesty, and actually making effort to *not* attract attention. We've all admired that type of person. What if, all of a sudden, she was puffed up with pride. All that was classy and positive about her would suddenly be crushed under the weight of the huge negative—the ego.

So what if it happens to you? If the "big head virus" strikes you, so what? The people who really care about you will still take you back after your head has shrunk with time, rejection or age, right? So what if you get a big head? So what, besides the fact that you've become a real jerk, of course!

Well, your bottom line is "so what." The fitness model communi-

ty is very small and crosses borders with the speed of an e-mail. Good people get talked about—and so do jerks, of either sex. Jerks don't get hired as much as good people. Is *that* enough "so what?"

The reason I mention this is because I've seen it happen—and I'm sure you've seen it happen too. So just be aware that the "big head virus" can happen to anyone, and learn to look at yourself as someone with the same fallible potential as anyone else. I have worked hard to avoid this at all costs.

Some of the greatest fitness models have the best attitudes—and their attitude is why they are great. They all *look* good, but Monica Brant *is* great. Mike O'Hearn is fun to be around. Christian Boeving is one of the nicest guys I have ever met. And I could go on and on.

Then why would you get an attitude over a 2"x 3" photo in the back of a magazine? If I've beat this dead horse completely, so be it. I apologize. But you get the point.

(from left) Bill Phillips, Clark, Anita.

Chapter 16—
Chances Are, You Won't be Laughing All the Way to the Bank.

I said it before and it is time to say it again. Most likely, you're not going to be in a position to quit your day job.

This chapter exists solely to burst your bubble so you don't put your notice in at the office! Say it to yourself, and start to make it reality in your mind (and heart). No matter how well you succeed with fitness modeling, your ticket to easy street is not likely to come somewhere on (or behind) the pages of a magazine cover.

Let me give you an example. I've been on several covers of several major publications and the most I have received for my mug and sodium-depleted physique was $500. People tend to *think* I have made much more, but that is simply not the case. The bubble bursting continues...

Let's look at it another

way. Assume that a full-page ad nestled within the pages of *Muscle & Fitness* magazine costs $20,000 in a revenue buy. I'm guessing here but I think I'm close (maybe even *underestimating*). Regardless, then how much would you think the front cover would be worth if *you* were to purchase it for an ad? Yes, a lot more than you or I could ever afford.

With that in mind, it's up to *you* to capitalize on the expensive ad that just showcased all that good bone structure and chiseled muscle you've been dying to show off. Now it's up to you to make it a showcase for the entire world to see.

Send that magazine cover out all over the place to anyone you can think of. Work begets work. The best thing you can do is to make your "moment in the sun" make *more* "moments in the sun" for you. Most people don't see it like I do. Make the most of it!

So don't complain about the chump change you got paid to do the ad. The true "cashing in" comes when you cash in on your moment in the spotlight! I know for a fact that a lot of people would actually pay to get on the front cover of any magazine. You very likely may be one of them!

So with every bit of exposure you're fortunate enough to get, put it to work for you and turn it into money and momentum.

Of course, the way to do that is to exercise your common sense and return to the self-promotion tools we've been over and over in your "ritual for success." Your hard work has put the world where you've always wanted it to be. If you want to "taste" that again, get moving!

Chapter 17—
But Clark, How Can I Get an Endorsement Contract?

Go out and do something!

First, I don't suggest you waste the time of the supplement manufacturers if you don't have any credentials. And you don't necessarily have to go out and get your personal training certificate (although educating yourself about such a big part of your life is certainly not a bad idea).

The competition is stiff for contracts. So if you aren't an IFBB pro or a top level fitness competitor, chances are, you won't appear on the next box of *Met-Rx*. There are some people out there (whom you read about and know by name) who can't land a contract. So why would a multi-million dollar corporation give one to, frankly, a "no-name" (even to such a promising "no-name" as you)?

Realize, the only realistic way this can happen is if you win one of those high-profile fitness competitions like the *MaxFormation Y2K* by *Max Muscle*. By all means, give it a try. Give it your all. The process is the reward, even if it only leads to recognition from the people who care about you. And you could become an overnight fitness celebrity. If you're interested in *Max Muscle's Challenge*, call 1-800-530-3539 or log on to www.maxmuscle.com.

If you decide you want to go the competition route don't waste your time on competitions in your local areas (unless your local area is Southern California or Las Vegas). The only shows worth doing are the ones where you will gain the most exposure. For men, we're talking about *Muscle Mania* or *Super Body* competitions. For women, it will be the *Fitness America Pageant*. Both are promoted by *American Sports Network*. You can call 1-626-292-2222, or log on to fitnessamerica.com or musclemania.com.

You must be seen (once you're lean)!

Chapter 18—
Man Clark, I See You Everywhere!

Yeah, I hear that a lot—all of the time actually.

It is not because I'm any better looking or have a better body than you do. I'm no better than any other qualified model. I'm most likely just better at tenacity. The one thing I have is tenacity. I do not give up or let go. I knew deep down, long ago, that I had what it took. So I wouldn't (and couldn't) stop until I made it to where I am today.

Up to this point, I've been lucky enough to land over thirty covers. My good fortune has landed me in almost every fitness magazine in the world, appearing in possibly the most successful ad campaign the fitness world has seen (The New Theory of Evolution by *EAS*), healthy endorsement deals and two years as a guest host on *Kiana's Flex Appeal*. And all the effort culminated by allowing me to host my own national fitness program, *American Health & Fitness* (which, by the way, it is now airing internationally).

I know that it's sounds like I'm bragging, but I'm not. I know it happened and I'm not looking back—I'm looking forward! My point is that I pretty much made all of those things happen by never waiting for my phone to ring. And, of course, I made a habit of being smart and never being underestimated.

Many good-looking, wonderfully fit people expect the world to come and beat down their doors because they look so good. Hopefully, we've uncovered here that it really doesn't happen that way. But we've also uncovered the way it really does happen, too!

Maybe you have "it"—the special balance of physique and attitude, the magical equation and good luck that can lead to being a successful fitness model—maybe you don't. Who knows?

You know—if you take the chance and go for it. You'll never

know until you give it a try. And you'll only know once you've *given your try the best you have to give!*

Billboard in Hollywood on Sunset Blvd.

Lessons from the Other Side

Chapter 19—
Your Best Friend (If You're Smart): The Photographer.

By Rick Schaff,
Professional Fitness Magazine Photographer

I believe fitness modeling is the hardest type of modeling you can do. No other category of models work as hard to create perfection before the lens.

There are many factors that make a great health and fitness model. The best health and fitness models are the ones who are dependable—in every way. The following is my list of the ten most important tips to being a good fitness model:

1. First and foremost you have to be in shape!

And if you are not in shape, you better speak up before you show up and waste everyone's time and money. The only models that make any money in this field are the ones that stay in shape year round.

2. You must be well groomed in every way possible!

Your body must be clean-shaven to clearly show your muscular development and definition. This is very important! Your skin must be taken care of and be as blemish-free as possible. Your hair must be styled, cut in a way that enhances your "look" and compliments your facial features. Your nails must be cut and clean.

It is a good idea to always bring a bag with minimal make-up, hair gel, eye drops, a hairbrush, etc. Remember that every detail counts, and getting all the details right takes work, day in and day out!

3. You have to be on time.

If you continually show up late, people will stop calling you, no matter how good you look. This should be pretty straightforward, but you would be surprised how often it isn't!

4. Make sure your skin has enough color.

Whether the color is from a good tan, self tanner, or self-bronzer, you need to make sure it looks as natural as possible and as *even* as possible all over your body.

5. Always bring some comfortable clothes.

Just in case the photographer has nothing that works for your body-type and coloring, get into the habit of looking for clothes that fit you well and show off your body best. Bright, solid colors (red, blue, yellow, purple—but *never* white) usually work best.

6. Make sure to bring some food and water.

Be prepared with a healthy snack so that you have energy during the shoot. At times, you will be shooting great and really working the camera when all of a sudden your blood sugar dips. You will have to struggle to keep your energy up. It is important to be prepared. Your personality in front of the camera and your blood sugar are often directly related.

7. Bring some oil and a towel.

This is important in case the photographer doesn't have any, or used his up with another model.

8. Bring portable workout equipment.

You might want to bring some resistance bands so you can warm up quickly and easily just before shooting. A little pump is a great way to put the finishing touches on your physique.

9. Don't complain about every little thing!

Be a professional and realize although you might be exhausted at the moment, these pictures are going to last forever and you will be immortalized by them.

10. Communication is crucial.

If you are uncomfortable for any reason with the way something is going during the shoot, speak up and let the photographer know immediately! You need to work together to get the best shot.

About Rick Schaff

An avid weight trainer since the early age of twelve, Rick Schaff's strong beliefs about the positive effects of weight training, coupled with his intense desire to create, sets him apart from the rest of his colleagues. After receiving a BA degree in Cinema Arts from the Columbia College Film School, he worked as an Assistant Director on films while also working with top fashion photographers Firhooz Zahidi, Herb Ritts, and Wayne Mazer. For the last seven years, Schaff has remained focused on the art of physique photography and worked with the industry's top champions and leading figures.

Schaff has also established himself as a prolific writer, creating dozens of personalized training articles on professional athletes, as well as producing a monthly column called *California Muscle News*. He has also developed an online health and fitness magazine, www.healthandinspiration.com. Today, Schaff's work can be viewed all over the world in elite health and fitness magazines like *Muscle & Fitness, Muscular Development,* and *Oxygen.*

Chapter 20

Exercise Your Common Sense– And Keep Working!
(A Practical Perspective from Behind the Photographer's Lens)

By Martin Ryter

1. Are you ready?

Many bodybuilders come into modeling and try to adapt the modeling industry to their training routine. Their reality is that they are in shape once or twice a year, so they expect the industry to drop everything and photograph them. Everyone else's reality is that this is not going to happen. Bodybuilders who can be presentable only a couple of seasons a year might get in a few jobs, but they are not going to have a long, successful career as a model.

The professionals that fitness models get their paychecks from make *their* living creating advertising photos all year long. They cannot and will not wait for a model to get in camera-ready shape. They instead must use models whose bodies are ready 24/7. Therefore, you must commit to being in shape all of the time to succeed.

2. Paint-on tans don't cut it with me.

You will need a real tan without tan lines to work with me. The rub-on tans may look okay to the human eye, but film sees colors differently—and permanently—and the models that use rub on tans tend to look streaked, uneven and orange when the photos get to the publisher.

Rub-ons tend to look especially unattractive around the fingers and toes. Your hands play an important part in posing for photos. The only model I've worked with who has made rub-ons presentable is your mentor for this book, Clark. Maybe he's figured out what works for his skin tone. And he probably mixes his rub-on tans with a little time in the sun. He also knows he's coming to work for me, so he's turned the process into a science specific to his coloring. No one else has been nearly as successful for my tastes.

Finally, no tan lines are extremely important because you never know what kind of clothing you will be modeling. You just don't know what pose the photographer may have in mind. You may be asked to assume a pose that will show off a section of your physique that you never thought you would be featuring. We simply cannot deal with the possibility of a big section of your non-tanned skin hanging out.

3. Shut up (Please...)

It can be tough to be a photographer. We're all experienced in the process of shooting good photos. That's why we're hired and make a consistent living. But most of us didn't get our degree in psychology...

Photographers don't want to hear about your diet, your hunger, or your disappointment with your cuts on shoot day. It is also really uncomfortable for us when you beg for more jobs. We honestly don't want your opinion on poses either, or which kinds of shorts you feel you look best in. We don't care which angles you think are your best. We're the professionals, so you need to trust us. We'll figure out very quickly what your best angles are.

This will sound a bit harsh, but it's the truth: *a model is a rent-a-person, not a rent-an-opinion.* So to be blunt: *please shut up if you don't mind.* Do what the photographer needs you to do.

4. Watch out for offers from the public sector.

At a contest, you might find yourself being approached by several photographers and clients. Some will be legitimate. Most will simply have an angle; to get you to work for "exposure." "Exposure" simply means they don't want to pay you. Run.

When you do get an offer, never accept on the spot. Never give out your phone number. And never, ever pose for photos right then and there. Instead collect the contact information, check out the photographer's reputation and then call them, to either accept or reject their offer.

If you need to check someone out and do not know how, e-mail me at ryter@pacbell.net. I will help you.

5. Understand working nude.

Working nude is up to you. If you choose to do it, you will need to understand the three different types of nude modeling.

Art photography— This type of photo is one that tastefully captures you and is used in coffee table books, greeting cards and posters. It is safe and will not harm your modeling career.

Nude magazines like Playboy or Playgirl— These photos are much more sexual by nature and truly exploit all of your body for the world to see. Many top bodybuilders have appeared in these magazines. Some clients think this kind of modeling is fine and some don't. You will definitely lose some jobs because of this kind of exposure and you will definitely get some jobs because of this kind of exposure.

Erotic nude modeling— This is what you see in the adult industry. If you pick this kind of work, you will not be able to do any other kind of modeling or acting.

Never shoot nude with a beginner photographer. Never sign a photo release without a clear understanding of what the photos are going to be used for, written into the release you are signing. Also know that the law says that the original negatives, slides and prints are the sole property of the photographer. So be very careful.

6. Don't use up your publicity too soon.

For example, say four magazines want to use you on their covers. Hey that's great publicity that will lead to other jobs. Just don't do them all the same month. If you do all those covers at the same time, they obviously will appear on the newsstands all at the same time.

So what's wrong with that you ask? Again, it's true you will get a lot of attention and this attention will lead to other offers. But by using up all this attention in just thirty days (as long as the magazine is on the stand), you are killing your chances at long-term future work.

Client's want to use whoever is hot right now. So if you space your magazine jobs out so that you agree to shoot one each month, you end up on a new cover each of the four months. You will definitely have to rely on your day job to pay your rent, but you will also have 120 days of fame instead of 30. In effect, you remain hot much longer.

7. Have a standard haircut.

If you want to really make money as a fitness model, you need to understand that your hair is one of the things clients need to be able to make different. They definitely don't want you looking the same in their ad as you do in the ads of their competitors.

Remember that *the photo is not about you.* It is about some product, publication or service you are helping to represent. You are just a component used in the ad. If your hair is short and unchangeable, you are not versatile and you will lose out on many jobs. You need a flexible, standard model's haircut.

Also never show up at a shoot with a fresh hair cut. You will just look like you have a peeled head. In addition, never show up with your hair full of product and pre-styled for the client. Simply bring your hair preparation products and ask the client how they want your hair to look.

8. Watch your shaving rashes.

Unless your skin is unaffected by shaving (especially the abs and chest), shave only one hour before a shoot. *Never the night before.* You will get a rash, which means a retouching bill for the client. And this bill can be so expensive that it becomes not worth shooting you, so they send you home—unpaid.

9. Avoid tight waistbands or underwear.

Skin takes the shape of whatever is placed against it. These impressions can take up to an hour to go away. If you are in a shoot that depends on the sunshine and the sun goes down while the crew waits for your skin marks to relax, then *you* have blown the shoot.

So never wear tight elastic waistbands before or to a shoot. Instead choose loose sweats that tie at the waist. Keep them loose and do not wear underwear with them.

10. Be exactly five minutes early for a shoot.

Never come any earlier because you might interrupt the shoot ahead of you. And never be late!

11. Never bring anyone with you to a shoot.

The set is not a place for your visitors to be entertained. This includes girl/boyfriends, agents, managers, fans, other models, immediate or extended family, etc. No one.

12. Smiling pulls the abs tight.

Try it.

13. Stay off of stimulants on shoot day.

They make you too nervous and jumpy, which in turn makes the crew not want to work with you. They also affect your facial attitudes on camera negatively.

I suppose the bottom line is to do your homework. Prepare all the little details, like the ones listed above, so that you not only come across professionally, but you are also relaxed in front of the camera.

When you've done your homework and addressed all the details like a professional, you'll act, look and shoot like a pro. Good luck. I hope to see you in front of my camera.

On the set of "Flex Appeal."

Chapter 21—
The Five Secrets of Fitness Supermodels.

By Jason Ellis,
Fitness Model & Professional Photographer

Being both a professional photographer and model, I've collected more than a few insights over the years that I believe will help you achieve your goal of becoming a top fitness model very rapidly, *if you take action!* From a photographer's point of view, I've noticed that the top professional fitness models that I've photographed and have come to know seem to have many of the same common traits.

Five Secrets of Fitness Supermodels

SECRET # ONE: They are master self-promoters and networkers. Besides having agents trying to obtain work for them, they are constantly sending out photos of themselves or calling potential clients. They don't just wait for things to happen, they make things happen.

SECRET # TWO: They're 1000%—yes I said 1000%—*committed* to being the very best at what they do. You can just take a look at the way they live, and there is no doubt of what their main objective is.

SECRET # THREE: They have discovered their niche, where they fit in (and where they can stand out), and have exploited their assets! Top fitness models are also very aware of their competition and have figured out where they can be most successful.

SECRET # FOUR: They are "professionals." They show up on time, they are well-prepared, and follow up with a phone call or a card expressing their appreciation (this may seem like a small point, but let me assure you that a *"thank you card" is one of the most important ingredients to your success as a top fitness model).*

SECRET # FIVE: They have taken all the necessary steps to look their very best. In fact, they take extreme, even absurd measures to perfect key features that set them apart from everyone else. Top fitness models are action-oriented creatures.

Now, onto one of the most critical ingredients to your success—your photo shoot! Here are five tips that I believe will ensure successful pictures that will help "sell" you! (Remember that you've got to sell yourself in your *own* photo shoot if you're going to convince other people to pay you for *their* photo shoot!)

Top Five Tips For a Successful Photo Shoot

1. Prepare, prepare. Start preparing weeks—even months—in advance, for all the details that will affect the outcome of the shoot. Some things you will need to consider are the following:

- A good, even tan. The top fitness models I shoot always seem to have perfectly tanned, bronzy skin—with no tan lines!

- Professionally cut and highlighted hair (or shaved bald).

- Perfectly conditioned bodies (they never say, "Oh, it just looks like you need another week to burn off those love handles!").

2. Select the best photographer for the look you are trying to capture. Do your research. Ask around and choose a photographer on the basis of his or her work (also, someone who you have a good working chemistry with). Do not choose a photographer just because he is convenient, is your friend, is the friend of a friend, or is the friend of your cousin's ex-fiancé. You get the point!

3. Select the perfect clothing for the look you are trying to capture. The most important thing, in my opinion, is the way the clothes fit. Make sure the cut and fabric is flattering to your physique. Be sure the clothes are in good condition, pressed (if necessary), and definitely not faded! Also pick a color that flatters your skin tone and hair color.

4. Practice different poses with your body and different facial expressions in front of the mirror. Believe me when I tell you, top fitness models know themselves! They know each micrometer of their being, and how to hold each and every facet of themselves in just the right way to get the perfect outcome.

The mirror will help you in developing this ability. Once you receive the proof sheets from your shoot, examine the result of each of your photos carefully, then ask yourself, "How can I improve the next time I shoot?"

5. Cover the basics. If you don't have a professional make-up artist (which I think is a must for females), here is the least you can do: conceal the blemishes, and cover those nasty zits and razor burns. Use a powder that matches your skin tone to get rid of shine (use throughout the shoot as necessary). Tweeze (or, for females, preferably wax) your eyebrows.

Some Other Smart Tips:

- Female models should wax bikini lines and shave under arms. And speaking of underarms, don't wear that chalky, white deodorant (ever). It looks terrible, and it's a sure way to mark you as a rookie!

- Don't wear glasses 30 minutes prior to shooting (the eyeglass nose rests will leave indentations on your nose and the side of your face).

- Likewise, don't carry bags over your shoulders on the shoot. This will also leave lines on your skin.

- Bring hairspray and a brush on photo shoots to take care of "fly-aways," etc.

- Manicures and pedicures are also a must. (Pamper yourself, and the results will be evident in the way you shoot!)

On the set of "Ship Shape" with U.S. Navy SEALS.

Chapter 22—
The 'How' of Who Signs the Check: The Supplement Manufacturer and Magazine Company.

By Sean Greene, President of *Max Muscle*

Over the past seven years, I have worked with many fitness models and professional bodybuilders while preparing for catalog shoots and at various functions pertaining to our magazine, *Max Sports & Fitness*. I have seen examples of both shining professionalism and acute *un*professionalism. Unfortunately, I've seen more of the latter than the former.

Before I became president of *Max Muscle*, I was a competitive bodybuilder and worked with other industry photographers and companies. I observed how many of the models I worked with conducted themselves at these shoots, and it became obvious to me very quickly which ones would continue working and which ones would not. These observations, experienced firsthand while I was "in the trenches," gave me unique insight as to just how completely and profoundly unprofessional many professional athletes could be—and continue to be.

What amazes me the most to this day is that these shoots were their bread-and-butter, part of their living and a means of generating income, yet they weren't making the least amount of effort to be cooperative. Many of these models wondered afterwards why they weren't getting called back for more shoots. It takes a lot more than a pretty face or great physique to get the top photographers and companies in the industry to want to work with you. That is where professionalism comes in.

The following are a list of points that many other companies and I look for when considering working with a fitness model or bodybuilder:

Marketability—How does this person represent himself in public as well as in his or her private life? Does his look sell the particular company's product or the magazine's specific article?

Punctuality/Dependability—Does this model have a reputation for being on time to events or shoots? Is he or she dependable? Companies spend a great deal of money to promote events or coordinate photo shoots. Making sure they can count on the model or athlete to show up is imperative.

Attitude—This is probably the most important characteristic of all. Is this person easy to work with? Are they helpful on the shoot? Having a good attitude is essential if you want to continue working in this business or any other.

Compensation—This is also very important. When considering how much to charge for your rate, make sure to consider all of your options. What have you accomplished? Is there a demand for you? How recognizable are you? Are you comparable to others at your level? If you are having trouble getting work (or especially getting rehired), this may be something you have to consider.

Appearance/Grooming—Don't think you'll continue to get work if you show up to photo shoots or promotional appearances out of shape or looking slovenly. This industry is about looking good and exemplifying that image all year long. Obviously, there are exceptions for top professional bodybuilders who are preparing for their contests. However, if you plan to depend on making a living from the marketing side of this industry, you better make sure you look good when you are called upon for a shoot or promotional appearance.

Max Muscle has signed numerous athletes to endorsement contracts over the years and has found one thing to be true: *Most of these individuals do not follow through after they get the job!* They may be persistent before the contract is signed, but the only time we see them afterwards is when they come by to pick up a check or product.

A name or look might get you in the door, but it's what you do *during* your contract that counts. Word travels fast in this industry. If you are talking up a company's products or services, setting a good example, staying motivated and doing what you can to promote that company, they are going to want to keep you around for the long haul. On the other hand, if all you do is complain about how much you have to do for your contract or how you aren't making enough money, chances are your contract isn't getting renewed.

What we look for in a fitness model is someone who personifies what a healthy lifestyle consists of. Using models that are in shape and look good helps sell more magazines and supplements. We are no longer interested in signing someone just for the sake of having a name under contract. Good business has to go beyond that. And *good-business common sense* is now a matter of having someone represent us who best represents what *we* stand for in the industry.

Quality, professionalism, integrity and attention to detail are what *Max Muscle* represents in the market place. These are the same attributes we look for in the people we decide to work with. Of course we want our models to be fit, attractive and recognizable. But more importantly, we desire people who are easy to work with and flexible, ready and willing to adapt as the industry changes around them.

We are in the business of helping people by providing positive role models in our growing publication *Max Sports & Fitness*. You might not be in the position to be one of our models yet, but we have created an opportunity for everyone to have the same chance to be a fitness celebrity. Our publication is equally interested in showcasing people who have made the transition from frumpy to fit, as we are committed to the sport of bodybuilding that put us on the map. If you are interested in a career in fitness or desire to have a great, well-defined body, we may have just the opportunity for you.

We encourage those of you working to get in the best shape of your life and interested in becoming a fitness model to try the *MaxFormation Challenge*. If you think you are already in top shape, drop us a photo and resume. We are always looking for fresh, new faces to help us market our products and model in our magazine.

Just remember that it's not so much who you are as much as it is *what you represent!*

Sean Greene

Sean Greene is the president and chief operations officer of *Max Muscle.* He oversees all of its divisions, including Corporate Stores, Franchise Stores, Magazine Publishing, Sales and Marketing, Clothing Production and Supplement Manufacturing. Greene is also the associate publisher and editor of *Max Sports & Fitness* magazine, which has a worldwide monthly circulation of more than 75,000. Greene earned his Bachelor of Science degree from the University of Florida in exercise physiology with an emphasis in human nutrition and a minor in business management. Along with his partner Joe Wells, Sean was recognized in 1998 as Entrepreneur of the Year from the *Academy of Bodybuilding Fitness and Sports Awards* for the contributions they have made in the fitness industry.

Chapter 23—
How to Turn Your Dreams into Realities.

By Bill Lykins, Television Producer

What does it take to make it in "The Business?" As the CEO and executive producer for *SandStone Pictures*, it's my job to cast the perfect person or people for every project we produce. Whether your passion is television, print, or movies, there is an opportunity for you—if you know how to go about converting that opportunity into a reality.

Ask yourself this question, true or false: To make it as a male fitness model, you must be 6'2" with blond hair, blue eyes, rippling muscles and must have a masters degree in radio, television, and film? Or if you're a woman, true or false: To make it into the big time you must be 5'9" with eyes of blue and hair of the tinted blond variety, have a perfect figure and look incredible in a bikini? My experience—starting with the casting process and ending with candid feedback on every episode we've ever produced—is that these stereotypes are completely false.

These days, the entertainment industry touches virtually everyone on the earth. Therefore, common sense says that the entertainment industry must represent all people, from all walks of life, with a real need for talent of all shapes and sizes. The same holds very true for the fitness industry. Anyone who tells you different doesn't know what they're talking about.

So if I may, I would like to offer a few practical suggestions. First, don't forget the simple things that you may take for granted. Before you come to an audition, simply have a good breakfast, lunch or snack. Follow whatever ritual you have that ensures you have energy (this is *so* very important)!

And don't forget to brush your teeth—that could be a bummer right off the bat (remember your smile and your personality are the first things we see in the audition). Personality is often what decides who gets chosen, when the race for the role is particularly tight.

Secondly, dress for the part. And project an attitude to match your appearance. In other words, present the right "you" for the role you're auditioning for. If you were auditioning for the role of a corporate executive, you probably wouldn't want to show up in shorts. If you're trying out for a fitness show, nice, clean workout clothes would be the right choice (it might seem obvious, but I've seen people ignore the obvious more often than you'd believe).

Producers need to know exactly what they are getting, so make our job easier. For instance, for Clark's showcase television series *American Health & Fitness,* we were seeing hundreds of people and making some very difficult casting decisions in the process, while pre-production was still rolling forward at full speed. A small army of people you're not seeing at your audition are still crewing up and scheduling the entire shoot and post-production. They're finding locations and striking network deals and dealing with many legal issues. So if you do things to make our jobs easier, I guarantee your chances of being cast will be much better. In a way, your job is to make our jobs easier.

Do research before the audition. Learn about the part you're trying out for whenever possible. Be prepared. Whenever we're auditioning someone that we feel might have the right look or fit the part that we're casting for, I tend to ask a few questions relating to the part. For instance, if you are auditioning for a workout program, you really should know a bit about training and nutrition.

This demonstrates that you took the time to learn a little about the topics the audience is going to expect you to know something about, and it also gives us an opportunity to see how fast you think on your feet. This weighs heavily on my casting decision (you would be amazed how many fit people don't know very much about proper diet and exercise).

Work on your memorization skills. In most casting sessions you will be given a "side" (one or two pages of dialogue) to interpret and perform. It always impresses me when someone knows their lines or maybe glances down occasionally. That tells me that they are quick learners. It's not as hard as it sounds. Any good coach will tell you that it's not the words you deliver, but the thought behind the words that you're communicating—or "selling."

Additionally, I suggest you spend a little money to get a good dialogue coach (not necessarily an acting coach, but someone who works on how you deal with copy and playing yourself before a camera). Check a prospective dialogue coach's references with three or four talent agencies in your local area. If you plan on making a career from your talent, it's wise to invest a little money into it.

When you're in an audition and a producer or director gives you direction, that's a good sign that they're interested in you. Realize that you've been invited to collaborate on the spot, so take the direction thankfully. This is where all your preparation becomes invaluable. Be sure to listen carefully, then do your best to perform your interpretation of what you were asked to do, whether you agree with the direction note or not.

Finally, the most important thing I know to make it in the entertainment industry or any other industry is this: Have faith in yourself. If you don't believe in yourself, how can you possibly expect anyone else to?

Auditions are fairly high-pressure situations. It is very important to project a high level of confidence, in who you are and the talent that you have to offer. The way to project that confidence, in spite of all that pressure is to do your homework—in your physical presentation, your mental preparation, and in your appearance. Walk in with confidence knowing you have every reason to get the part!

These are the facts. You will run into rejection. Usually, even though you'll still beat yourself up, your rejection is due to so many factors that are out of your control. There will always be someone better looking than you and more talented than you. The good news is that none of that matters if you believe in yourself. Stay committed to your dreams at all cost, don't get discouraged and never give up. Believe this and you will succeed, I promise.

On the set with Jack Lalanne.

Chapter 24—
The Big Payoff.

I know this is the moment you have been waiting for—the contacts, addresses, and people who can help you get to the place of recognition. I hope you have read the entire book before you plunge into mailing your packets out. I can only give you the information. It is up to you to prove to everyone—and especially yourself—how efficiently you will put all this knowledge to use.

I was reminded recently by a friend and top photographer to please remind you not to waste money on expensive packages. I touched on this subject in an earlier chapter, but he insists that it is worth repeating. He recommends just sending the basics. He has often seen people spend a lot of money on great promotional kits when it just wasn't necessary. It is the same lesson reiterated throughout the book—*get in the habit of being smart!*

Below is a list of the names and addresses of some places where you will most likely want to send your information. Most of the information I provide is easy to obtain; it is just a matter of doing the work. Guess what, I did it for you. I figure it's a fair trade for investing your hard-earned money in this book. So here's the payoff.

First, let's look at a few of the top fitness magazines. Some of the best advice I can give you is how to find the information yourself. That way, if I failed to list a specific magazine you want to contact, you'll know how to get the information yourself.

Go to a bookstore and head to the magazine section with pen and paper in hand. Open the magazines of your choice to the first few pages and find the information about the editors on staff—and start writing (and if the people that work there get upset, you didn't hear it from me)! Write the name, phone number, and address of the art director. That will be your contact person for the magazine. Simple, eh?

While you are there, look for the names of the contributing photographers. Most magazines contract out photographers. Some will be employees, but most photographers freelance. Once you have those names, simply look them up on the Internet. We live in the Information Age—take advantage of it!

Now that I have taken out some of the legwork, here are the magazines you will want to contact:

All Natural MD
150 Motor Pkwy
Hauppauge, NY 11788

Muscle Magazine Intl.
Oxygen
American Health & Fitness
for Men
5775 McGlaughin Rd.
Mississauga, Ontario Canada
L5R 3P7

Ironman
13450 S. Western Ave.
Gardena, CA 90249

Natural Bodybuilding
Exercise for Men Only
350 5th Ave. #3323
New York, NY 10118

Nutri Mag
7710 Balboa Ave. #117
San Diego, CA 92111

Muscle Media
555 Corporate Cir.
Golden, CO 80401

Muscle & Fitness
Mens Fitness
M & F for Her
Shape
21100 Erwin St.
Woodland Hills, CA 91367

Physical
320 N. Larchmont
Los Angeles, CA 90004

Max Sport & Fitness
1550 S. Sinclair St.
Anaheim, CA 92806

Send your information: *Attn: Art Director.*

Yes, there are many more magazines. And several more are guaranteed to continue coming out every year, at least for the near future. And with each of those new publications, the need for more people like *you* increases.

Here are some helpful tips from Kerrie-Lee Brown, Editor of *American Health & Fitness for Men* magazine:

"I receive hundreds of packages from models daily, and I take the time to look at all of them. However, the ones that really stand out for me are those that include an in-depth bio and resume including the model's experience with print work, television and special appearances. Also, I congratulate those models that send professional comp cards and any additional portfolio photos that suit the fitness theme of our magazine, as we like to keep them on file for stock images. It's always a pain to have to send back comp cards and personal photos because we may not remember what you look like for future assignments. A cover letter is also crucial, and don't forget your correct contact information. You'd be surprised how many models send in packages addressed to the editor with the wrong return information. How are we supposed to get a hold of you if we're interested? If the model has read *American Health & Fitness* and knows what kind of photos and models we're looking for, that's great too."

So now that you have a start with the magazines, let's move on to the photographers.

Most of the photographers on the following list work on a freelance basis. This simply means they are contracted out by specific magazines (usually several) to take stock photos, either given a model to shoot or asked to choose their own. These are also the people who will get you seen internationally by sending packages out to the foreign publications.

Again, there are many more working photographers. Just look in the magazines, find the names, and locate them on the web. Here are a few words of wisdom from Joanne Fierstein, the agent of David Paul, a premiere photographer in the industry:

"The bottom line is the visual aspect. I understand photography and realize that sometimes photos aren't

Rick Schaff
649 Oxford Ave.
Marina Del Rey, CA 90292
rschaff007@aol.com

Ralph DeHaan
P.O. Box 615
Cardiff, CA. 92007
760-634-3310
Dehaanphoto@home.com

Jason Ellis
P.O. Box 916
Laguna Beach, CA 92652
949-278-7171
www.jasontv.com

Alex Ardenti
8117 Manchester Ave. Ste. 57
Playa Del Rey, CA 90293
Ardenti@pacbell.net

Jim Amentler
8117 Manchester Ave. #573
Playa Del Rey, CA 92093
jim@jimamentler.com

Michael Neveux
13450 S. Western Ave.
Gardena, CA 90249
www.ironmanmagazine.com

Joanne Fierstein
(David Paul's agent)
14011 Roblar Rd.
Sherman Oaks, CA 91423
818-905-1930

Martin Ryter
Ryter@pacbell.net

Robert Reiff
P.O. Box 11301
Marina Del Rey, CA 92029
www.robertreiff.com

an exact representation of how good someone really looks. So if you are sending a photo to me or anyone else in the industry, make sure you are relaxed while being photographed. The camera picks up nervousness, yet it will also pick up your true beauty if you are relaxed. Make sure the photos you send us are the ones you love the most, the ones that let me see *you*. Women, don't feel the need to be too ripped. I like to see a combination of femininity and muscularity. It is a fine line. And be sure to include all of your contact information so that we can follow up with you. I look forward to seeing your photos. We are always looking for new faces and great bodies to shoot for various magazines. I wish the best luck to everybody."

If you are interested in getting television exposure, I suggest that you call your local news station and volunteer your time to do a fitness segment. Prepare and plan a list of segment ideas, locations, workouts, etc., prior to making the call. You may even suggest a regular two-minute spot that could air once a week during the newscast that needs the most help (most likely the afternoon broadcast).

Now that you are armed with everything you need, what you do with it is up to you!

Chapter 25—
Agencies: Work With Us, Not Against Us...Please!

An Interview with Jeff Donaldson

As mentioned earlier in the book, I have had a hard time finding anyone who can match my energy to help me succeed in the business of modeling and television. Perhaps I even badmouthed agencies.

Recently, I came across an agency that made me realize that I may have been a bit harsh. So I guess I owe an apology to my new agents at *Pacific Model and Talent* in Redondo Beach, California. I have finally found a group of guys and gals who get me out there as much as I get out myself. I guess the lesson I have learned is that sometimes it takes a while before you find one that you have synergy with.

Having said all of that, I thought it would be beneficial to interview Jeff Donaldson of *Pacific Model and Talent* to give you the straight scoop on how to land a great agent and how to make the relationship beneficial to both parties.

CB: Jeff, how long have you been in the business?

JD: Seven years.

CB: What is the best way for a complete novice to find an agency?

JD: These days you can go online and find almost anything you want. If you are in a major city, you can go to the bookstore and ask one of the clerks for an agency book or publication.

CB: When someone finally gets an agent, what are they expected to provide?

JD: If someone is interested in acting, we will need a black and white 8"x 10" headshot. The look (of the photograph) should have mainstream appeal. If you are interested in modeling, we will need a ZED card. This card will include one nice photo on the front and four different looks on the back such as one sports look, one business look, one body shot and one other shot that shows you off the best.

CB: Tell me about the "model searches" I hear about on the radio and television. Are they legitimate or a scam?

JD: I'm probably going to upset a lot of people, but almost all of them are a scam. If anyone asks you for money, it is a scam.

CB: How much should someone pay for decent headshots?

JD: That is a hard question to answer because photography is an art. How can one put a price on that? I would give a rough estimate of $25.00 to $100.00 per roll. But it depends on the photographer and whether or not you want the negatives.

CB: What is one of the biggest problems you encounter working with models/actors?

JD: Dependability. Many models and actors do not seem to treat this endeavor as a career. Treat it like you would a normal job. If you are called for an audition, show up on time, have a great attitude, be positive, and be relaxed. I think that if more of my talent pool treated this like a real job, they would surely have a much higher success rate.

Another thing I recommend is living close to the area where you will be called to most often. For example, if you live in San Diego and most all of your calls are in Los Angeles, remember that you will have a total of four hours minimum on the road. Most auditions will last a total of five minutes. Now tell me, will you want to do that four to five times per week? As harsh as it sounds, most of that traveling will be for nothing. It is a tough business sometimes. An agency doesn't ever want to hear, "Oh, I can't make it today." We make money when you get hired. We want you to work; therefore, we will send you out as often as possible. You will get more auditions when we see that you are dependable, motivated and willing to pay your dues.

CB: What would be some tips or suggestions you would have for a beginner?

JD: If you are interested in acting, get some acting lessons. Be prepared. Try to stay busy. There are many ups and downs in this business and people tend to get discouraged. You have to create a positive image, despite all of the negative possibilities. Also, be confident in yourself. Just because you don't get hired on a job doesn't mean you don't have what it takes. When you walk into an audition or casting session put everything else on the back burner. Forget the traffic, the fight you had with your significant other, or anything else that will take away from your winning personality. You have about 30 seconds to show them that you are the answer that they have been looking for. If there is copy to read, know it. Be confident in how you look. Act like you have been in this situation a million times before. Never let them see you sweat!

CB: What are the qualities of the people at your agency who get the most work?

JD: As I mentioned before, dependability, optimism, and confidence.

CB: How much should someone expect to pay an agency per job?

JD: If it is a union job, the agency receives 10 percent. For modeling jobs, the agency receives up to 20 percent.

CB: Is there anything important that you want to add?

JD: When an agency gets a job for you, please treat us with respect. If the client tries to hire you again behind our back, please don't let them. You will be tempted so that you don't have to pay our fee, but fair is fair. We initiated the relationship; therefore, we should be involved in the transaction in the future. And remember it is our job to get you higher rates. It is impossible for us to do that if you cut us out of the process.

CB: What words of encouragement can you offer to those who feel they don't have what it takes to make it?

JD: I doubt this will boost someone's confidence, but if someone doesn't feel they have what it takes then they probably don't. People move to L.A. everyday aspiring to be a star. More than half move back within the first year. Basically, you have to be tough and stick it out. Develop your skills in both acting and modeling. Be prepared. Don't be fooled and think your good looks will make you the next superstar. If you really want to succeed, persevere and eventually you will find your niche.

Clark and Rebecca Mullins on American Health & Fitness.

Chapter 26—
Tips for Being a Successful Fitness Model.

By Kelly Hanna,
Art Director of *Physical Magazine*

I've worked in the fitness industry for the past three years, and I've dealt with models from one end of the spectrum to the other. The great ones always seem to have the same attributes that stand out and make me want to hire them over and over again. To name a few, they have positive attitudes, the willingness to work hard on any type of photo shoot, and they stay in top shape throughout the year so they can always be counted on, even at the last minute.

The ones that I have had bad experiences with never get called again, no matter how good they look. Bad experiences come from dealing with those that have serious attitude problems. They show up late to a shoot, bring friends with them, complain about things there is no control over (such as the weather), bug you about wanting the clothing from the stylist, and get moody when they didn't order enough lunch and they're hungry again. (If you need to eat like a horse, I suggest you bring a cooler with you so you have enough to eat throughout the day.) And on top of all of those things, the worst is when a model tells you he can get ripped down in time for the shoot and he shows up looking the same as he did in your office three weeks ago. That is a complete waste of everyone's time and money, not to mention it makes the model look like a complete idiot, and that's a good way of not getting hired again.

What I look for in a model, besides the obvious, which is a good look and exceptional physique, is an overall good attitude and desire to work hard in order to achieve the best possible outcome from a shoot. It's so pleasing to work with a model whose goal is in tune with mine, which is the desire to create images that will not only complement the model but will inspire those who see them. In order to achieve this, it takes good art direction, great photography and a model's effort to do whatever it takes to make the shot. That means working hard on a shoot. Sometimes the shoots can be long and draining and other times it's outside and the weather conditions aren't ideal, but you still need to keep a good attitude and realize that hard work pays off when you put the effort in.

There are several ways I find the models that I use. I have found that the best way of finding models in the fitness industry is through word of mouth. For example, I will get calls from models I have worked with in the past referring new models, or I will work with people on shoots and they'll tell me about the model they worked with the day before. That's a great way of finding new people, because sometimes the best models aren't with an agency; they just find work through networking.

I seriously believe that networking is the best way to promote yourself. If you want to get your face out there, you need to go to the events and the shows and meet people and *put your face out there*. The key to having people remember you is to have a great attitude and personality. If you look fantastic and you act like the world should bow to you, it's not a great way of getting people to hire you, especially if you are new on the scene.

I worked with a guy recently who was seen in a show and approached by one of our editors. I hired him for a shoot even though he had never modeled before in his life. Come shoot day, he had an attitude the entire time. First, it was the fact that he had to drive too far for the shoot (which was because he lived outside of L.A.), then the studio was too hot, then he was hungry and it wasn't even lunch time yet! It was one complaint after another. For someone who is a complete unknown and has never had a modeling job before in his life, he's on the wrong road if he thinks he can survive in this industry. Needless to say, I will never hire him again.

Another way of finding models is through modeling agencies that represent fitness models. They send me zed cards of different models, and if one stands out, I will call them in to meet them and take a Polaroid for my files. Sometimes zed cards are deceiving because the photos were taken the year before and their body doesn't look the same or their hair has changed. If you are with an agency, I suggest that you constantly keep your card up-to-date with your look. It's really frustrating to call in a model from a card and have them come in looking nothing like the card. That's a sure way of not getting hired. Even if your body has changed and you tell your agent, often times they don't relay that to art directors and will still send you on the call.

A great way of finding models is also by seeing them in other publications. I may see the smallest photo of someone, and if I like their look I will make sure I find out who they are. So if you are trying to get seen, don't think that a cover will be your only way of getting noticed. If you think that you are too good to do small jobs, think again. Sometimes the smallest jobs are the ones that lead to the big ones.

Now, here are a few quick pointers to help you when you do get a modeling job:

1) Ask if there will be a hair and make-up person at the shoot. If there will be someone at the shoot, then show up with clean, gel-free hair and a clean, make-up free face. I always hire a hair and make-up person when shooting a girl, but sometimes for men it's not necessary. If there won't be a groomer there, you should bring a comb and some lotion, to give your skin a nice glow.

2) Don't apply Protan without asking if you should. I am one of those art directors that hates Protan. It's messy, it looks orange and if you're shooting up close workout shots and the hands are showing, the palms look awful with Protan residue on them. There are many other tanning lotions available that give you an even, natural-looking tan, without that awful orange look—find them.

3) If you need to leave the shoot at a certain time for whatever reason, tell the person booking you *before* the shoot. It's really irritating to get to a shoot and the first thing out of a model's mouth is "When will we be done? I need to leave at two." When you're hired for a full day, that means nine to five, and sometimes later than that. So if you have plans, make them known at the time of your booking.

4) Practice posing in front of the mirror and get comfortable with

yourself. Find the ways that your body looks its best. Which side is better, if any? Practice how to stand and pose. Practice different facial expressions, smirks and smiles. It will help you tremendously if you know how to hold yourself and know which looks work for you. It's pretty awful to work with stiff boards who are in the business of looking good and don't even know how to hold themselves in a pleasing way or smile right. Just practice in front of the mirror. Trust me, it will help you. Above all, if you believe in yourself and have the confidence to get yourself out there and not give up, success will prevail. Keep working hard on your physique and keep the right attitude, and when you get to the point where you think you're ready to get out there, give me a call.

From the Horse's Mouth

Chapter 27—
Fitness Modeling:
A Woman's Perspective.

An Interview with Monica Brant

People often ask me how I got into fitness modeling and how I have been able to make a living in the industry. First and foremost, I tell anyone who asks that I give thanks every day for my good fortune and consider myself very blessed.

Secondly, I've always looked at everything I've done as an opportunity. I always let everyone I meet know that *I'm here and willing to work.* And I always have my promotional materials ready—my resume, pictures, cards, etc.—to back up my sincerity and enthusiasm.

However, I think that everything has to have its limits. You need set your limits and know exactly what you're *not* willing to do to land a job. Some promoters consider "performance appearances" a form of exhibitionism, so I've had to explain that I'm not that sort of model. In some situations, I've been forced to refer to contracts that my manager has locked into place before I've even arrived.

While that's not a form of modeling I'm interested in, there's a lesson to be learned in that experience as well. I remember when I was first getting started in the business that some girls tried to act "slutty" in an attempt to draw attention to themselves. At the risk of sounding preachy, that didn't work then and it really doesn't work now. It tends to attract the wrong sort of attention.

I count myself very fortunate. I've made some lucky decisions and I've been able to build a career by landing some of the "holy grails" of our industry. I've enjoyed the perks that come with getting several magazine covers, a steady booking of year-round appearances, and landing a great sponsor endorsement contract. Since "how" to be successful is the reason you're reading Clark's book, I'll outline how it happened for me, so maybe you can take some of

those lessons and find ways to make them work for you.

I've never really sat down and said, "This is what I want to do." When I got started, I never thought I'd be making all those appearances and selling all those pictures. I was very lucky. I started out when fitness modeling was just beginning. I figured out what worked (and what didn't work) and I evolved with the sport. Back in the early '90s, I didn't have a higher goal of where I wanted to be today; but now I know I want things that weren't as important in the beginning of my career. I want to have kids—it's the time in my life to fulfill that side of my personality.

Fitness competitions were my "in" into fitness modeling, which evolved hand-in-hand with getting into the magazines. It was probably no coincidence that things started going well in fitness competitions around the same time I started landing magazine covers. In hindsight, there was a synergy there. Competitions helped me get covers while the covers gave me some visibility with the fans at the competitions.

Covers are great because they create momentum. They generate interest, which can lead to endorsements. Get it in your head that you *can* land a cover. You *can* enjoy success in the appearance and competition sides of the industry. You *can* obtain—and maintain—a reasonably lucrative endorsement contract. In my opinion, it all has to do with your attitude.

I'm in my third year with *Universal Nutrition*, my contract sponsor. Through them and for them, I attend a variety of bodybuilding events and functions for signings and appearances. I also pursue work outside my sponsorship requirements, modeling and making additional appearances to make a comfortable living, as well as my little "cottage side business" of answering requests for pictures and autographs. And I advise and design exercise programs for clients via my website, www.monicabrant.com.

An endorsement contract is a great thing to have in this industry. But once you get your sponsorship contract, that's just the beginning of your responsibilities. With my sponsor, *Universal Nutrition,* my commitment is not just about the sponsor wanting to use my picture in ads. They like me to be at contests and events. I represent them and I take that seriously, and I think it is that commitment that has allowed me to stay with them for several years.

Whether I travel for my sponsor or for myself, I do a lot of two-hour fitness seminars. I'm hired to go to a lot of gymnastics facilities, gym openings, store openings and one-year store "re-openings," bodybuilding shows and events. I sign pictures, give general advice and answer questions.

People ask me most often about how I got into fitness, but they usually have deeper questions. Everyone wants to know something different. Often, I try to just get them to talk about themselves. Eventually, they start to open up and ask the real questions they have.

For instance, a recent appearance engagement I attended was a one-year anniversary (or "re-opening") for a gymnasium. The owner's thirteen-year-old daughter was at the event. Obviously I was there to build business for the gym, but the owner also wanted me to talk to his daughter and give her advice on being active in sports and taking care of her body. By the end of the two hours, I'd gotten her to ask me questions and I could see she was excited, as well as her whole family.

I often come across situations like that when I do appearances, and I really enjoy that side of the work. I enjoy the one-on-one aspect, working with people and helping them out. Obviously I've got to make a living, but my appearances afford me the opportunity to spread the word about a clean and healthy lifestyle.

I used to be hired to perform fitness competition-style, gymnastics-heavy routines at appearances. However, I do not focus on making performance appearances anymore, either in competition or at fitness seminars. It no longer makes sense for me the way fitness competitions have evolved. Now the majority of girls at the top fitness competitions have really strong gymnastics backgrounds. These are girls who have been training in gymnastics since they were six or eight years old and have great routines. I think my gymnastics is solid, but it's only a part of the package I offer.

If you really get serious about fitness and you're hired to make appearances, you may be expected to perform, which is great if gymnastics is your strong suit.

I've been very fortunate. I tend to get booked almost every week of the year. I've recently had to say "no" to some work simply because I'm overbooked and can't physically be in two places at once. I hate to admit this, because I know it will sound a little pompous, but I'm *so* fortunate with the amount of work offers I get that it's a real luxury to have a week with no job bookings.

I do my best to get into a weight room three to five times a week, juggled between appearances. And I really try to get a cardio workout four to seven times a week. My favorite cardio activity is running. I find it as much a form of relaxation as I do a necessary exercise. My favorite place to run is on the beach, which is obviously one of the perks of living in Southern California.

How I Broke In

So how did I get into fitness modeling? For me, breaking in has been an exercise in patience. Fitness competitions were the route I took and they really were a great way to break in.

I've been training for fitness since 1991. About a year before that, I started competing in bikini contests. Bikini contests gave me a sense of being on stage, and how to present myself in front of a crowd under the pressure of competition. Strict bikini contests can be a good way to prepare yourself physically and mentally for fitness competitions and fitness modeling.

As far as competing, I really started making serious headway in 1993, while still in Texas (my home state). I met photographers and I always had my stuff ready—my promotional materials, resume, etc. As I said earlier, whenever I met people, I let everyone know that "I'm here, and I'm willing to work."

When fitness competitions were first getting started, there was no *IFBB* (*Joe Weider's* International Federation of Bodybuilders, which presents the *Ms. Fitness Olympia* contest, among others). It was just a handful of girls who got together in the very beginning.

I stayed around for an extra day after one of the events and I got to shoot with top photographer Ralph DeHaan and fitness model Dennis Newman. We shot in Dallas for *Muscle & Fitness* and I ended up getting the cover. That sure didn't hurt as things started to come together.

In 1995, I was competing more frequently in fitness competitions and realized that if I was going to compete in fitness seriously, I should be in California. I also realized I needed more quality gymnastics in my routines, which helped prompt my decision to move to Los Angeles.

Like I said, I'm really not a gymnast—or at least not a lifetime gymnast like a lot of the girls successfully competing as the sport has evolved into the new century. Of course, there are ways around not having a strong gymnastics background. You have to work to present yourself and come up with ways to show off your unique attributes, physical skills and personality.

I had been out in L.A. for only about a week when I competed in the *Fitness USA* competition. Shortly after the competition, I received a call from *Jan Tana*, who had a new fitness competition that involved all the top girls. I was very fortunate and won the *Jan Tana* show. It was my first win in fitness competitions, which really started everything moving. Because I was a fitness competition winner, I was invited to compete in the first *Ms. Fitness Olympia*. I came in seventh place and went pro.

From my effort in the *Ms. Fitness Olympia* and *Jan Tana* competitions, I was asked to model for the *Jan Tana* catalogue at a shoot in the Bahamas. I don't know if it was being prepared and putting myself out there or just simple good luck, but something was working.

In 1995, I did a couple of pro shows as an *IFBB* pro. Now I had appeared in articles in all the magazines. In the summer of 1995, right after I did the cover of *Muscle Magazine* and right before I won the *Jan Tana* competition, I started getting calls. Although there were only two shoots on my resume, I again had the opportunity to shoot with *Muscle & Fitness*. Then Kiana called from *Kiana's Flex Appeal* on *ESPN* and asked me to be a guest trainer on her show for a season. The momentum began to grow as the appearance opportunities became more and more frequent and I got more and more photo shoots.

Fitness competitions are a great way to get into the fitness modeling industry because they teach you proper ways to diet. They also teach you dedication and patience, and how to push yourself to a higher level. It's a simple equation that can lead to success in our industry: *Contests plus magazine visibility equals momentum.*

I'd encourage you to make a name for yourself in the contest circuit, while you continue to consistently keep your name out there in the fitness community. Of course, you can't expect to become a great fitness competitor in just a week or a few months. You have to really work at it in the gym and in all other facets of your life as well. Go to a nutritionist to learn how to eat right. Work on your performance skills and the best ways to "show your stuff" in front of a crowd. And work on training correctly to peak for competition. That is a crucial skill to develop because it will also give you the experience you need to look your best for photo shoots.

One thing to remember about competitions is that you don't have to win. I won in 1995 and didn't win another competition until 1998, with *Ms. Fitness Olympia.* You've just got to stick it out. The key to fitness competitions and fitness modeling is to stay in the game. That's what keeps you visible and in a position to take advantage of related opportunities that arise.

While fitness competitions are a good way for girls to go, it is important to realize that you shell a lot of money out to do a *Ms. Fitness Olympia.* You will spend money in this industry on trainers, choreographers, wardrobe, travel, special diet considerations and many other small expenses that add up very quickly. So maybe just do a few shows. I actually began in bodybuilding and progressed from that discipline into fitness modeling.

My Break-In Strategy

I don't want to lead anyone to believe that you *have to* start out in fitness competitions to get work as a fitness model. And you don't necessarily need to be in Southern California either (at least not when you're getting started). If you've made good progress, send a flattering photo and a letter to the art directors at the magazines you wish to target.

You'll want to take some casual photos and really review them, to find out what your weak and strong points are on film. Then take more photos with a professional photographer, and find an agency to get you started.

You can take your first batch of "test" photos to an agency and they can also rate you. They'll usually have photographers they like their clients to work with that they can refer you to. (Otherwise, they may demand that you spend money on even more photos from a photographer who specializes in a look that the agency prefers for the people they represent.)

If you plan to pursue the fitness competition route and live outside of California, you can enter regional contests. Look for regional modeling and commercial work to help you grow accustom to the techniques of working under pressure in front of people.

So when you have photos that you're happy with, and you've gotten good feedback on those photos from a variety of people (including agencies and professional photographers), it's time to send them to the magazine art directors with a cover letter. In the letter, let them know that you are interested in fitness modeling and *interested in their magazine*. Besides telling them a little about yourself and what you do, recount a short success story. Above all, make sure it's *your* story. Then use your success as a springboard, a transition to explain how you and your talents are a good fit for their magazine.

Start attending fitness and bodybuilding shows. All the best working photographers are in front of the crowd near the stage. They can help move you forward very quickly. They often get assignments and are asked to hire the models themselves. Or they'll simply refer a good fitness model prospect to a magazine art director.

So if you're at a fitness or bodybuilding show and you want to break into fitness modeling, be visible—not only to the photographers, but to the powers that be: magazine editors, art directors, and clothing, supplement and equipment company representatives.

Do your homework. Talk to people at the booths and at your gym to know *who* you need to know. Have business cards—or (even better) photo cards—ready and on-hand. Make sure you have something to hand these very valuable contacts.

Then, create some way to follow-up with them. I've opened doors (and kept them open) in this way. My best advice is to be brave and get out there.

Fitness Model Realities

When you're getting started, you'll feel the need to take modeling jobs to get experience, to get professional photos of yourself and to create a feeling of momentum.

From the beginning of each booking, if I don't like the way a job is evolving and I don't like what they're asking me to do, I refer back to my contract. And I've always had a contract since day one. You should too, even something as simple as one page that outlines exactly what you'll be expected to do and wear.

I've been very, very lucky. I've done well and I don't take anything for granted. However, there are some hard realities you really need to keep in mind.

First of all, I don't think working as a fitness model pays as much as it should. For instance, if I do a photo shoot for *Muscle &*

Fitness, the shoot may only pay about $300. Sometimes that's for a day that starts at 8:00 a.m. and may finish as late as 9:00 p.m. And that's one of the best paying publications.

Certain magazines pay no money at all. Others don't pay because they use freelance photographers, but the photographers will sometimes pay you. Again, as a reference, *Muscle & Fitness* and *Muscle & Fitness Hers* each pay around $300.

The problem with trying to make a career out of fitness modeling is that you are competing with many girls who are willing to work for free. At most levels of fitness modeling, you're realistically looking at a day rate of no more than about $100. As far as a viable career path, it's just not worth it. But that doesn't mean it can't be a part of a broader strategy.

Appearances offer the chance to make substantial money and a decent living. However, it takes time to build up enough notoriety for people to pay to fly you to their gym or event, put you up and pay you a decent appearance fee.

I work weekly, which means I've managed to make a career out of this. That's rare. What people don't realize is that it took me nearly six years of hard work to really set it all up. You have to be patient and things can get pretty lean while you're building up momentum.

Now that I'm doing well, I'm rarely home. So recently, I've started scheduling fewer appearances. I know that may sound like I'm not grateful for the notoriety I've achieved in the fitness industry, but I've finally allowed myself to have a relationship. That may sound a little odd—that I actually have to schedule enough time to have a nice relationship, but it's true.

Soon after things began to pick up for me as a fitness model, competitor and spokesperson, I realized that everything tends to have a price tag. You feel a demand on your time with training and traveling, and you'll end up making sacrifices in your personal life and with personal relationships. It can become difficult with frequent appearances to maintain a relationship and make time to work out.

To give you an example, I take a lot of redeye flights and I have very little time to get into the gym. I'm lucky if I get to train, which obviously can be a problem since I make my living by being in shape year-round. It can get a little crazy when my schedule gets tight.

Let's say you're on the East Coast for an appearance. You try to squeeze in a workout before catching a redeye back to California. Your plane lands as the sun is about to come up. You have a day to try to re-acclimate to the time change, do your laundry, get in a workout, sleep and call the people you care about. Then, the next morning, you fly into a new town at 11:00 a.m., do an appearance, and try to squeeze in a quick workout before getting on another red-eye flight.

Don't get me wrong: it is very exciting and I love the work! But my point is that it has its difficulties.

In addition, there's very little crossover from fitness competitions and modeling into other parts of the entertainment industry, especially for women. Kiana and Corie have both done movies, but they're already television personalities.

In other industries, people tend to look at female bodybuilders as a little too extreme. It's getting better, but it's still evolving. Maybe *you'll* be the woman who makes a name in fitness and breaks into television and film!

Don't get me wrong: the attention and notoriety you can receive in this industry is nice. It's a privilege to make a living that revolves around taking care of myself and helping other people take care of themselves. I get paid to be an inspiration for people to engage in a better lifestyle. I think that's a big part of fitness competitions, and why they're getting more and more popular.

Finally, many girls trying to break into this industry are operating on misconceptions. You *must* have a fallback career plan, unless you have a rich husband, of course.

You need to be absolutely honest with yourself. Some girls are told the wrong things by people who may have ulterior motives. You may also have a great look, but maybe you're a little too pushy. That may work for some people, but I've always found success in treating people the way I'd want to be treated, and from simply talking to as many people as I can, especially at the major events.

Like I said, it's important to have a long-term strategy with consistency—consistency of communicating with the right people and consistency in your effort to make your body better.

My Future in Fitness

This is my first year not competing in fitness competitions. I am very excited about my newest endeavor, the next big challenge I have in my life—starting my own *IFBB*-sanctioned fitness competition.

The competition will be an annual fitness show in Washington D.C. It will be an *IFBB* national pro qualifier, a path to bigger shows like the *Ms. Fitness Olympia.* Competitions have been very good to me, so I see this as a way to give back to the industry with a quality show. I will also allow me to remain a part of an industry and community that has become like a family to me. My hope is that the show will be something I can keep working on every year, possibly even becoming a premier event over time.

I'll continue to maintain my website, offering web shopping opportunities and personal training services to clients around the world. And I'll also continue to make appearances because I love working with people from all parts of the country.

In all my appearances, I have noticed that after people ask me how I started (and succeeded) in fitness modeling, they often ask me how I've managed to stay in the game for so long. For me, it's been important that I place my trust in God, stay positive, meet people, make sure I have people on my side that can protect me, and just adapt to what comes my way.

A good place to begin is to simply jot down what you've accomplished. That will start your own positive momentum, which will help you stay on a positive track when you're weathering the rough spots (because there will be rough spots). But there will also be great, very rewarding times too!

Clark and Monica Brant

Chapter 28—
It Pays to Know Your Craft.

I know many of you will seek other work in addition to doing fitness modeling, and I highly suggest you do so. There are other gigs out there that you can and will get in due time, but always remember to be consistent with every job.

Most professional shoots, outside of the fitness world, will pay an hourly rate with a minimum time requirement. I just came from a job that paid $150 an hour for a two-hour minimum. Not the best rate, but not a bad one either. Not many professions pay $150 an hour to someone who is basically just standing there. Although I am now back at home, I am still getting paid for the shoot because I nailed the shots quick. It pays to know your craft and practice your skill on jobs like these.

I was actually a replacement for another guy who didn't "cut the mustard" on this job. I walked in knowing exactly what would be required of me. In other words, I did my homework before I went to the gig.

I knew I was going to be modeling costumes for a Halloween catalogue. I called my contact at the shoot and asked her what costumes I would be modeling. I was told that the costumes would be Spider-Man and Space Ghost. Then I looked at a comic book to see how Spider-Man poses. I practiced four Spider-Man poses, went in and basically "nailed it." We got the shot in five minutes. I could hear everyone on the set commenting on how they had wondered how Spider-Man would pose, and how good I was at it. Well, guess what? I knew, and my preparation made the shoot easy for them. Then I did the same with Space Ghost. I was out of there in fifteen minutes with a $300 paycheck (minus agency fees). And guess who will get the call the next time that they need a superhero for their catalogue? You got it—me!

The next positive thing that can happen is that my agency might get a "we loved that guy" call from the catalogue. Then my agency will work harder for me because they'll know I am a professional model and take my trade seriously. We get paid to be who they are paying us to be. The faster and easier we become who they want us to be, the faster we make money and the easier it makes their job— a true win-win situation.

Practice your skills, do your homework, be on time, be professional and get the heck out of there as fast as you can. Everyone will be happier at the end of the day. I know my family is. Now we can go to dinner tonight while a less prepared model would still be there sweating it out and then fighting rush hour traffic on the way home, adding *another* sixty minutes to their day.

Another Spider-Man shoot for American Health & Fitness magazine. I spent seven hours in make up!

Chapter 29

Mastering Interviews, Auditions & Castings.

By Brett Matheson

Throughout my career in fitness modeling, I found the most important aspect to getting work was my ability to master interviews, auditions and castings.

I have personally experienced the audition and casting process literally thousands of times and throughout the years have consulted many newcomers. I have also worked behind the scenes as a production assistant and have conducted various casting sessions for national commercials.

Believe me when I tell you that your ability to present yourself well at interviews, auditions and castings is perhaps the most important skill you will need to develop in becoming a successful, working fitness model. I hope to familiarize you with this process by providing definitions, examples and exercises to assist you on capitalizing on your abilities.

As a result of my vast experience, I jumped at the opportunity to participate in Clark's book and to contribute to your future success.

Basic Definitions and Situations

Interview— Sometimes called a "go see," this general meeting gets you acquainted with the photographer, casting director, art director, client, or anyone else in the business who may be in the position to book or select you for a job.

Casting/Audition— For commercials, a casting director will typically audition around one hundred people per day. As a rule of thumb, the audition is usually videotaped and sent to producers and directors where the selection process continues. A few models will receive a "call back" for the final selection. Note that national commercials pay considerably more than most print jobs. It is advised to prioritize commercial auditions when scheduling your appointments.

On print jobs, expect to present your portfolio and leave a comp card. Be prepared; you may be asked to model a swimsuit or another article of clothing for a fitting. Also, you may be combined with other models to see how you look together.

Script— This is the text of a show or screenplay. You may request to view a copy prior to your audition to familiarize yourself with the role you are auditioning for.

Sides— These are portions of the script. When auditioning for many commercials, TV shows, videos and movies, there may be sides with dialogue or physical directions.

Preparation

Do your homework— Get all of the detailed information for your audition correct the first time. This will save you hours of frustration. Here is a list of some important questions to ask: Who is the client? What should you wear? Do you need to bring a specific article of clothing, such as a swimsuit? Is there suggested parking? Do you have an appointment time or is there an open time range? Do you have the exact address and will you need an up-to-date detailed map? For those of you in the Los Angeles area, a *Thomas Guide* can be your best friend.

Be on time— Allow plenty of extra time for delays. You may have just spent an hour in traffic and arrived 15 minutes late only to find that everyone has gone to lunch or the session has finished. You are left with a missed opportunity.

Appearance— Learn what clothing and colors compliment your look. It is important to be comfortable with your image. Study yourself in the mirror. What colors go best with your skin tone? Play with all your images and get a good feel for what you can present.

Remember, white and shiny clothing tend to reflect the strong set lights and appear hot and glowing to video cameras.

Tools

Your three basic marketing tools on auditions are your composite, portfolio, and commercial headshot. As a model, you are in the business of self-promotion. Nobody can promote you like YOU! These marketing tools are a direct reflection of what you have to offer. You will need to constantly update and build your tools by adding new shots.

Composite— Also called a comp or zed card, a composite is typically a 5"x 7" printed compilation of images with a headshot on the front and collection of images to show your range as a model on the back. This card will contain your name and agency contact information, as well as all of your measurements and stats. This is your primary marketing tool. Your agent will use this to submit you for jobs. This acts as a calling card for photographers, art directors, casting agents and other potential clients. This also gives them something they can put on file for future reference. Always carry a stack with you.

Portfolio— This consists of twenty to thirty 9"x 12" photos and magazine tear sheets that show a variety of looks. Your agency will provide you with a portfolio with their logo on it. Your agent will also provide you with lists of photographers to shoot with and advise you on how to layout your book.

Commercial Headshot— This is generally an 8"x 10" black and white photograph. You will want to show lots of smile and personality for this one.

Journal— Prepare a journal or notebook. Make a section titled "Contacts." Put as much detailed information as you can about everyone you meet in the industry: names, numbers, addresses, e-mail, birthdays, and any notes of interests. You never know whom you will need to follow up with or contact in the future. It's a small industry. There is a theory called six degrees of separation, where statistics postulate that you know every person in the world through somebody who knows somebody, etc. You will find the world of modeling small and interconnected. These people are the key players in your career. Many will mix well in your social life. In time, you will develop an impressive list.

In your journal, prepare another section titled "Inspiration." This is where you will set your goals, make observations and direct your career.

> *Examples:* Write down helpful questions such as, "What is my ultimate goal as it relates to fitness modeling?" Discover your motivations by asking, "Why do I want this?" Write all your responses down. "What are my weaknesses? What areas do I need improvement in? How can I improve them? What are my strengths? How do I see myself? How do I think others see me?" Continuously ask yourself questions. For inspiration, go through magazines and cut out ads you feel you are best suited for. Ask yourself, "What are these images trying to say? How can I effectively communicate this when I go on auditions?" Make similar observations on commercials, television shows and movies. Nobody said this would be a no-brainer. Your results will improve based upon the continued work you contribute.

Attitude Adjustment

Attitude— The best models exhibit a high level of emotional intelligence. More specifically, they must interact well with others and relate to all sorts of different people in various situations. A good habit is to treat everyone equally and with respect. Watch out—that assistant you thought was nobody may actually be the producer, who has the final say. Stay away from gossip. Intelligent minds discuss ideas while small minds discuss other people. You can be sure anything you say about someone will eventually make it back to that person. It's been my experience that models that go into auditions with a poor attitude don't last very long. If you go into this business complaining about conditions, putting people down and draining everyone's energy, you are in for a very humbling awakening.

I recently starred in a comedy film called *How to Become Famous,* in which my character, Todd, becomes famous. The film is a parody of typical characters you come across in this industry. Todd is portrayed as a stereotypical cocky model that is conceded, snobby and backstabbing. Everything comes easy for him based on his looks and body. Eventually he hits the big time only to have a rude and embarrassing awakening in the end.

In real life, Todd's character wouldn't make a successful model. His personality would hinder him at interviews and auditions. Body and looks are not enough to go the distance in this industry. More important than looks and opportunities in this industry is the way you deal with things. Always keep your attitude in check.

Stress— Even if you have done your homework, you may find yourself facing stressful situations like traffic, parking, weather conditions, crowded waiting rooms and finances. All of these can take a toll on you. Your ability to manage and overcome stress at every casting is crucial. When you find the challenges of stress affecting your attitude it is a good idea to have some techniques to help balance you out.

> **Deep Breathing Can Help.** Close your eyes and concentrate on the flow of your breath. Keep concentrating on the flow until you feel a sense of calmness. Most stress is associated with events from the past. By focusing on your breathing, you shift your attention to the present. Practice this technique and notice the effects. It works!

> **Don't Bring Stress With You.** Another useful technique is to pack all stressful thoughts inside an imaginary suitcase and leave it outside the door. Allow yourself a break from any stressful thoughts. Notice how light you feel not carrying that heavy load into an audi-

tion. Be creative and invent ways to maintain your best.

Affirmations: Creating affirmations are good strategies to help overcome stress and difficulties. Affirmations are most effective when framed in a way that evokes a feeling.

Examples: I enjoy modeling. I am honored to be at this audition. This interview feels great. I feel in tune with this casting. I feel perfect for representing this product. Create some of your own heartfelt affirmations and write them down in your journal.

Establishing Rapport— Getting a conversation going is essential to building associations and relationships. Do not brown nose, or present over-the-top sweetness. Be sincere, be real, and be yourself. Humor is a fantastic tool; it breaks down defenses and warms people up to you. A quick wit will show your personality. The client may open conversation about you or the job. If so, great. A conversation will also allow you to show your personality. Relevant and sincere questions about the job at hand are encouraged. Occasionally there just isn't the time to get acquainted. You may be rushed in and out. Don't take this personally.

Rejection— Every model must learn to deal with rejection. It is part of the business. Go into the casting and do your very best in the moment. Once you leave the audition, it is important to "let it go." You've done your job and now it's time to look toward your next audition. No amount of hoping or worrying will help you afterwards. You will sleep better at night by putting it in the past. Let every job you get be a surprise.

Competition— Looking at competition is a good thing. Variety is necessary in modeling. Competition helps you grow and drives you to develop yourself. A successful model is motivated by the desire to achieve, not by the desire to beat others. Eventually you will work on jobs with your competitors and they become your friends. Don't be surprised when another model helps you by recommending you to an agency or a photographer or even a booking.

Dealing with the competition can be more difficult at times. Invariably every model is faced with waiting room chatter. Many nervous models will unconsciously practice their art of self-promotion by expounding on how much work they've gotten, trying to reassure themselves by letting you know and just how great they are. There are also those who have made an art of psychological sabotage. With stabbing comments such as, "What are you doing here?," "I'm surprised you got called in on this one," "Gee, you haven't gotten any work in a while have you?," "Can I see your book? You look really old here," or "Your look just doesn't seem to be in style right now."

Let's get a perspective on these personalities. Models who exhibit these behaviors see you as a threat to their survival. Politely excuse yourself from these conversations so you can focus on something more positive. Do not play into their game by taking it personally. Do not let these tactics disrupt you. One technique is to find the humor in it by imagining that you are holding up a mirror toward them and they are really speaking to themselves. See these individuals as your teachers of how you never want to act.

Confidence— Clients tend to look for someone who is self-assured and whom they feel can best sell their products. Before a model can sell a product, he must be able to sell himself. Pay attention to how you come across. Cockiness can appear as compensation for insecurity. Notice the tone of your voice and your posture. Do they communicate confidence?

Putting It All Together

Here is a common scenario with situations you may find yourself facing. You've signed in, filled out your casting profile sheet, and an assistant has most likely taken a Polaroid headshot of you. The other hopefuls are coming and going. Mentally stressful circumstances are overcome by focusing on a positive mental attitude. From out of the adjoining room you hear the casting director call for the next applicant. You gather your things and enter the magical room.

This is it—your chance to shine bright. Utilize any nervous energy by converting it to a pleasurable, heightened sense of awareness. Remember, your attitude is crucial. Be flexible for any changes they may throw at you. Pay close attention to any directions given. Usually you will be greeted. A handshake may be extended. If so, greet them enthusiastically and introduce yourself. Use your common sense, tap into your intuition and you will do fine. Give your very best.

In the process, you may spend an hour trading cooking recipes or a quick three minutes with a hello and good-bye. Either way, don't take getting the job for granted. Sometimes you've already got the job before you even showed up; they just wanted to see if you look like your picture. You just never know. Don't stress and enjoy the process to the best of your ability.

Keep improving, keep adding to your journal and you will learn the art of mastering interviews, auditions and castings. Now get out there and break a leg!

Clark, Jason and Brett.

BRETT MATHESON has been in the fitness modeling industry for 10 years. He has appeared in over one hundred commercials, fitness magazine covers, national campaign ads, and music videos. Some of Brett's industry clients include *Calvin Klein, Nike, Adidas, Reebok* and *Weider* publications.

He has been represented by *Ford, Wilhelmina, L.A. Models* and *Boss* and has worked in the Los Angeles, New York, Paris, Milan, Barcelona, London, and Hong Kong markets. His acting credits include a recurring role as a lifeguard on the television series *Baywatch* and a lead role in the soon-to-be-released feature, *How To Become Famous.*

Chapter 30—
Looks: A Blessing or a Curse?

By James deMelo

The story of my youth is the similar to that of an ugly duckling. In grade school, I was skinny and homely with a mouth full of braces. The only attention I got from girls was their laughter and I was the target of every bully's pranks.

Then, while I was in high school, something miraculous happened; hormones and hidden genetics kicked in and I went from obscurity to national prominence. Suddenly, pretty girls everywhere were interested in me. However, I still felt ugly and insecure on the inside. Beauty is truly only skin deep. Unless you are beautiful inside, no amount of achievement will give you fulfillment.

Instead of using my attractiveness to motivate and encourage others, I used my looks to manipulate, abuse, and advance my personal agenda. The only person I cared about was myself. Pride became the source of my personal defeat and was quickly destroying my future.

It was at that time that I found God. I was able to reverse the curse and see the real purpose for my looks—to be used for God's glory. Today, I am a good husband, a father of two, and have a thriving international ministry that works with people of all colors, backgrounds and social statuses to help them become beautiful from the inside out.

"Never pursue the passing at the expense of the permanent."

Modeling

Modeling was not something I aspired to growing up. When I started winning prominent bodybuilding contests, modeling jobs just came to me. I did not have to go through the grind of composites, calls and agents. My career, though short by choice, was a very successful one. It was a product of being in the right place at the right time. However, I had to learn a lot about the business. Here are some simple but helpful hints I recommend:

Read, read, read! I cannot emphasize enough how important it is for you to read anything and everything on the subject of modeling. There are many good books out there that will give you insight into the modeling world.

Study photos of successful models that are in your field, but don't limit yourself to just your field. Study other types of modeling as well. When you study the photos, study hand positions and body language, as well as facial expressions. You will be amazed at how much this will help you when you are in front of the camera.

Practice in front of the mirror. Smiles, hand positioning, profiles, and angles are all things that can be improved through practice. Learn to move and flow naturally.

Finally, pay attention to details. Maintain your hair, nails, teeth, and skin. It is important to keep all these elements in top form.

When you have done your homework and prepared for a photo shoot, your confidence will come through to the camera and you will take beautiful photos every time.

Chapter 31—
My Personal Code of Conduct for Promotions, Trade Shows, Contests, and Public Appearances.

I have been at many public events as a paid "celebrity." I have worked with some people who were great and others who weren't so pleasant. How you conduct yourself at an event is an important part of increasing (or limiting) your public appearances.

I try to be as flexible and helpful as possible. For example, if I am doing a grand opening for a nutrition store as a "celebrity" to sign pictures, I call the owner a couple of weeks prior to the event to introduce myself and offer any promotional assistance. While I realize that people look up to me, I certainly do not think I am better than anyone else. I help in any way that I can. I send copies of my show that they can play in advance, send advance photos for fliers, or give suggestions and encouragement to the people setting up the event. Keep in mind that the more prepared the promotion, the higher the turnout for the event. And the more people at the event, the better you will look.

Calling the organizer a few times demonstrates my commitment to the project. Prior to the event, I decide whether I want to give my photos away or sell them. Although I realize that many people make a great income from photo sales, giving out my photos adds value to my appearance. Everyone wants something for free. You can use it as a tax write-off. This is an individual choice. You may prefer to sell your pictures.

I always get nutrition and training questions at appearances. I always give people my full attention, regardless of how many times I hear the same questions, such as, "What do I need to eat?" Even if I know the person asking the question will never put the information to use, I still give them quality time. People are there for you to make them feel special, and it is a direct reflection on you and your reputation.

Remember that the goal of the promotion is for the storeowner to make money, not lose it. If they are paying you to be there, work for your money. I never feel that just by attending, I have done enough to earn my wage. I always make it my goal to help increase sales for that day. If someone asks me my recommendation for supplementation, I walk him to the shelf and sell him what he needs (after I have determined that it is needed, of course). I will never sell something just to make a sale—never!

I have helped storeowners have record sales days by staying longer than the agreed upon time in order to reach a certain goal. This is just how I feel it should be done. Go above and beyond the call of duty. Make a statement of what you represent in the industry. Either you will just sit at a table and sign a few photos or you will contribute to the success of the day. It is your choice.

I have been called back to the same location on more than one occasion for additional events because of my work ethic. Make the most of every situation and you will get the most mileage out of your connections. Either way, word gets out. People will highly recommend you to other stores or you will wonder why your phone has stopped ringing. Be on top of your game at every public appearance and you will have a long and profitable career.

Chapter 32—
Fitness Model Contests.
A Look at Indigo Man 2000, James Williams

So far in this book, I have tried to provide you with the best tips and advice on being a fitness model. Covering how to get a job, what to expect when at a photo shoot and the overall general nature of the business, you should be well on your way to starting a career in the business. Just remember not to quit your day job—yet.

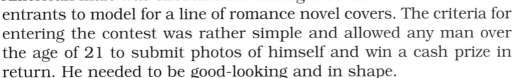

Now it's time to look at fitness modeling from a different angle—from a professional business that hires fitness models. *Genesis Press* is a romance novel book publisher based in Mississippi. *Genesis Press* prints African-American romance novels, but has also used a variety of interracial, Asian, and Hispanic models to fit particular characters in the past. The year 2000 marked the first *Genesis Press* *"Indigo After Dark"* contest, in which an African-American male was chosen from among a list of entrants to model for a line of romance novel covers. The criteria for entering the contest was rather simple and allowed any man over the age of 21 to submit photos of himself and win a cash prize in return. He needed to be good-looking and in shape.

Fitness models live in all places of the country and photo shoots may take place in any city. Therefore, to reach a larger audience outside of Mississippi, *"Indigo Man"* advertising was broadcast on the local radio stations in Washington, D.C., Atlanta and New York City. *Genesis Press* has a website, and the contest information was posted online with hopes that more interest would be drawn. Entrants ranged from bodybuilders to experienced fitness models to average everyday guys. Visitors to the site were encouraged to view the list of contest photos and vote for their favorite *"Indigo Man."* Each visitor had the opportunity to vote one time per week. At the end of the contest, James Williams, a technician from Atlanta, was declared the winner.

An Up-close Look at James Williams
Indigo Man 2000

For those of you who are beginners, James Williams is a good example to follow because he has only been in the business since 1996. Prior to the *"Indigo Man"* contest, James only had a few minor jobs as a fitness model. One of those jobs in particular taught him a lot about the business. He was doing a photo shoot for *Direct Wire* magazine, posing for a line of winter jackets. Overall, the experience went well, but when it came time to be paid, the check was not in the mail for several weeks. Although he finally did receive payment for his work, James now believes the wisest thing to do before accepting a job is to thoroughly research the company.

The same advice holds true for agencies. If an interested representative requests money up front, do not use him as an agent. The bills will start piling up before the agency even finds you a job. James believes the best way to promote yourself is by creating your own website and through self-promotion. If your resume, portfolio, and head shots are all online, you won't have to worry about an agent misplacing your information, having it lost in the mail, or spending lots of money to have copies made. He also recommends not having an agent. Agents are beneficial in that they will help find you jobs you may never be able to find yourself. On the other hand, James feels that fitness models can work at their own pace if they represent themselves. Often, they even hear about more jobs because they are looking out for themselves. An agency represents several models and doesn't necessarily pay attention to your individual needs. The longer you work in self-promotion, the greater your knowledge and understanding of the industry will be.

When James entered the *"Indigo Man 2000"* contest, the only fitness modeling experience he had was through his job with *Direct Wire* and a *Fubu* modeling competition, which he won. In fact, he was originally declared the runner-up, but due to the winner's arrogance and poor attitude, James was then chosen as the winner. "The judges really liked the way I worked the crowd. I just acted like myself and had a good time," he said. That's the exact reason why the people of *Genesis Press* enjoyed working with him so much. He didn't even complain when they asked him to do extra work without pay. I cannot stress how far a positive attitude can take you in this business.

Because James is an African-American, some of you may be wondering whether he lands more jobs than other models. "The opportunities seem to be coming my way, but next month may be a different story," he said. "Working as a fitness model really depends on the circumstances of what jobs are available, how persistent you are, and how hard you want to work at being a part of the industry." One of the reasons opportunities may be coming his way is because he takes care of his body. He follows a strict diet of mostly baked low-fat foods and plenty of fruits and vegetables. He also spends up to five days in the gym each week toning and strengthening his muscles—what dedication!

James has definitely found that by working hard, the benefits are greater. Seeing his body on the cover of a line of romance novels is certainly one of them. He does, however, know that becoming a success story is not that easy and he's taking everything in stride. Currently, he holds two jobs: he is a technician at *Verizon Wireless* and he also has created his own company called *One World Management Group*. His company is designed to help fitness models, actors and actresses, and people who want to promote themselves but are unsure how to do it. Once the company goes online, anyone will have the opportunity to post his own resume, photos, writing samples, or head shots. James is putting his philosophy to great use and hopes that aspiring models will benefit from it. Helping others become greater fitness models is really important in this industry because it's not about competition.

"Traditionally, when a model is needed for a cover shoot, the author of the book will describe what the character should look like. He then forwards the criteria to the photographer and the model is selected based on the author's decision," said Diane Miller, editor at *Genesis Press*. The *"Indigo After Dark"* contest followed those basic guidelines, but left the ultimate decision up to the general public. "Although the number of contestants could have been higher, I believe the contest will become a great success as more people decide to work as fitness models and visit the *Genesis Press* website," she added.

As a reward for winning the contest, James will not only be the cover model for *"Indigo After Dark,"* but will appear on six covers throughout 2001. "We couldn't have been more pleased with James," said Miller. "He was very cooperative at the shoot and very polite." Presenting a good attitude, even after long hours shooting photo after photo, really pays off in the end. James has flown to several cities to promote *"Indigo After Dark"* and also attended the *Romantic Times Book Lover's Convention,* representing both the novel and *Genesis Press.* His job may sound wonderful, but for all the work he has done to promote the novel, James has only earned $500. It doesn't sound like a lot of money, but the publicity that goes along with it can really be what you need to boost your career.

HotSkins Contest

Another great way to be seen in the fitness community is to enter the *HotSkins* model search. This contest is seen by everyone and is completely legitimate. Everyone must enter the model search to appear in their catalogue, regardless of how successful they already are in the industry. Rules, applications and prizes are available on their website, www.hotskins.com.

My only suggestion would be to put your best foot forward. Do not just grab a few pictures and haphazardly throw them in an envelope. Take your time and choose wisely. Make sure your head-shot is the best shot that you have. In addition, include a body shot that is innovative and different than anything they have ever seen. Imagine how many photos of great bodies they have seen; make

yours stand out in the crowd. The bottom line is to be extremely happy with every shot you turn in.

Now, arrange them in a nice folder with your essay and send it off in a *FedEx* package. As I mentioned earlier in the book, it just looks much more professional when sent *FedEx*. One word about your essay: Try to be humble and appeal to their objectives—to sell more clothing! They don't care about how hot you are. Be humble and assure them that by choosing you, it will help them "sell more clothing." Again, it isn't always about the model, it is about what the model can do for the client.

Even if a clothing company doesn't run a model search, I highly recommend that you repeat this process with every manufacturer out there—*Max Muscle, Body Alive, Perfetto, Hot Bodz, Crazy Wear, etc.* Most all these companies can be located by finding their advertisements in magazines.

Another great site for aspiring models is www.mensperspective.com. This site offers tips, articles, and contacts to help you get started. You can post your portfolio and they offer an online modeling contest too.

I also recommend that you search the web for online fitness modeling agencies. One great site for male models is www.mosaic-models.com. Check it out and submit your photo. It can't hurt to have your best photo online with several different fitness modeling agencies. If you get too many calls that would be a great problem to have.

Chapter 33—
Your Future is Now!

Having the information and taking action are two different things. I encourage you to take action today by starting from the beginning—and working through the process. Then, if and when need be, start all over again—from A to Z.

I can't tell you how many times people have asked me to give them exercise programs or nutritional advice, expressing a burning desire to get in shape, only to see me the next time not having changed a thing.

Knowledge without zeal is useless. Let the information you've just read take the trip from your head to your heart. Then take that great leap into action!

You *will* experience success—perhaps in ways you have never even thought of. Perhaps the degree of success that you experience will only become apparent in hindsight. Perhaps it will be a success grounded simply in knowing you pushed your body to a new level of conditioning or your resolve to a new degree of tenacity.

That success will be most rewarding—in tangible results and with regards to your self-esteem—if the actions you take begin in your heart.

You don't need to read too hard between the lines to see that the information provided in this book can apply to any area of your life. I encourage you to refer back to this information whenever you feel the need for motivation.

Get out of your comfort zone! You've done your homework. Take action, venture out and see where the adventure takes you!

Allow room for rejection, mistakes, fear and frustration. Even welcome these seemingly negative events and attitudes. They are the natural byproduct of your push to take on and (eventually) overcome new challenges! I have experienced all of these "negative" feelings in the past, and I'm sure I will again. I have not let the process stop me thus far—and don't plan to let it in the future.

Try not to focus too intensely on the big picture, so you don't miss all the fun along the way. You will meet new and exciting people that will add to your life and experiences with each small step along the way. In the event that the "step" you're on is the last step you will take forward in your progress, be sure you can look back and know you enjoyed the process as much as the reward (then you'll get to enjoy it all again)!

I hope this book has given you direction to pursue a career in the fitness industry. I mentioned earlier that chances are, you won't get rich. That is probably true, however, many people have evolved from fitness models to enjoy success in other areas of the business. Take this book for example. I am now an author! Go figure. I have enjoyed the benefits of success and have been able to support my family for years solely on my income from the industry.

Remember that people will look up to you and value what you do and say. Be an encouragement. Touch the lives of the people you meet in a positive way. Don't ever take what you have for granted and enjoy every day of it while it lasts. I can almost guarantee that if you do, it will last longer than you ever anticipated.

I hope to someday be working with you on a job and to have you tell me you read this book and it helped you make inroads into the exciting world of fitness modeling.

We'll share a bottle of water before they call for us before the camera to get that perfect cover shot—before the sun burns bright into the glistening Pacific Ocean...

Part 4:

Clark's Fitness Model Workout

Chapter 34—
My Simple Approach.

I've studied some of the greatest minds in the fitness field and have come to a simple conclusion: Be consistent, be smart, and be patient! Too many people try to over-analyze this basic concept. First of all, fitness should be enjoyable. Next, it shouldn't require a Ph.D. in physics to design a program that suites your needs. Yes, there is science behind it, but let's not overcomplicate the issue.

This has been my approach to achieving a magazine-quality physique. Rest, exercise, and proper nutrition are the most important elements. If you are natural (steroid-free), which I am for the record, rest is an important element that is often overlooked. Many enthusiastic trainees make the common mistake of over-training. So, rest if you need to and try to get eight hours of sleep a night if possible.

For some, training can seem confusing because of the many conflicting theories. One method suggests circuit training, another cardio, descending sets, or one set to failure. Don't waste time arguing over gray areas. There is validity to all of the theories. The key is to find what works for you. Of course you will need to study the benefits of each program, but don't let the abundant options overwhelm you.

Nutrition is what sets apart the serious fitness model from the average athlete. I have seen people train diligently only to justify a pizza for lunch. This will not land you any magazine cover, trust me. I suggest hiring a professional nutritionist. I have relied on one for years. While I know how to eat properly, being accountable to someone else increases my odds of success. If you don't know of a nutritionist, e-mail me and I will recommend someone to you. Believe me when I tell you that this is something that has taken me to the next level of fitness.

Now that you have the basics of rest and nutrition, let's get to the area you are really interested in—exercise. This is the workout program that has landed me on over 30 magazine covers (and counting), my own international television show, television commercials, and endorsement contracts.

Actually, you will probably be surprised at how basic my program is. Again, it is the combination of the above mentioned elements that really makes the difference. While this workout is simple, I do change exercise variables such as tempo, weight selection, angle of execution, size of handle, and the type of bar used. Most all these exercises are done at eight to twelve reps and three to four sets. I select a weight that will allow me to do at least eight repetitions, but no more than twelve. This repetition range is generally the most ideal for hypertrophy.

For all the exercises in this program, I recommend 8 to 12 reps unless stated otherwise.

Monday—Chest

Flat Dumbbell Press— Warm up by doing 15 to 20 reps with 50 lbs. Then, progress to 8 to 12 reps at 70, 80, 100, 120, and 130 lbs. (on a good day).

Incline Dumbbell Press— Since I am already warmed up at this point, there is no need for another warm up set. This is a common misconception. Continue with 80, 90, 100, and 120 lbs.

Weighted Dips— Be careful performing this exercise. It places a great deal of stress on your shoulder capsule. Perform 50, 60, 70, and 80 lbs.

Push-ups on Wobble Board— This exercise will be a new challenge for many of you. I use a special wobble board, or a flat, round board mounted on the top half of a hard ball. This causes an "unstable environment," which forces you to slow down your rep execution and results in a different neurological response than traditional push-ups. Give it a try.

Tuesday—Back

Pull-ups (forward, reverse, neutral)— Pull-ups can be done almost anywhere and have the best overall effect on the back. I perform as many reps as I can using each of the various hand positions, progressing from hardest grip (forward) to the easiest (neutral). Weights are not necessary because you are using your own body weight as resistance.

Closed and Open Chain Exercises

There are two different types of exercises—the **closed chain** and the **open chain.** A closed chain exercise is when you are pushing your body away from something (push-up or squat) and an open chain is when you are pushing something away from your body (bench press or leg press).

Pull-Down— This exercise is performed by pulling the bar down in front of you to approximately upper chest level. I start with approximately 100 lbs. and work up to about 160 lbs. As with every exercise, I *use strict, slow form.* I will either perform two or three sets with a forward grip or I will rotate with one set of each grip—forward, reverse, and then neutral. Variation is the key to most all of the exercises I do. Never get stuck in a rut.

Rows— This exercise can be performed on either a machine or with dumbbells. I rotate by performing bent rows on some days and machine rows on others. There has been an ongoing debate as to which is more effective. My opinion varies depending on the circumstance of the person seeking advice. The bottom line is to do something!

On the machine, I warm up with 100, and then move onto my sets of 150, 170, 190, 240, and 250 lbs. When performing bent rows with a barbell, the weight will be a bit lighter—135, 150, 185, and 200 lbs. Be careful to use proper form if you perform bent rows with free weights. Keep a slight sway of the lumbar spine and bend your knees about fifteen degrees to activate the strong glut muscles to stabilize the lower back.

Hyper Extensions— I like hypers for the lower back although some experts feel it places too much pressure on the lumbar spine region. Be careful! Generally, I start with no weight for fifteen reps and increase from there. I usually grab a 45-pound plate and perform four sets of 10 to 12.

Wednesday—Legs

Squats— To squat or not to squat, that is the question. So many people tell me, "Oh, I don't squat anymore." My response is, "WHY? Do you ever have to squat to pick anything up during daily activities? Then why not strengthen yourself in that area?"

I start by stretching with an empty bar using the same motion as the squat with weights. In fact, this is my theory for all stretching—to stretch mimicking the same activity you will be doing, hence stretching the exact muscles you will be working.

Then, I progress to 135 lbs. for two sets and increase the weight from there to 185, 225, and 315 lbs.

Lunges— I love the feeling I get from doing lunges! This exercise is great for the gluts. I start with a 50-lb. barbell on my shoulders and walk for approximately 50 yards. Then I move onto 60, 70, 80, and 90 lbs. I don't always make the 50-yard trek, but the idea is to challenge yourself by going as far as you can.

Leg Press— Always start your workouts with the most strenuous or unstable exercises first. Otherwise, you risk performing the exercises that require the most concentration and attention to form when you are tired. Leg presses are a great exercise if performed correctly. Be careful not to come down farther than the lower back will allow. Lower until you feel your lower back lifting off the bench. Your back should remain in contact with the back pad at all times! I measure my weight by how many plates are on each side. I begin with two plates and increase to three, four, five, and six plates.

Each plate weights 45 lbs., totaling 45 x 12 (six plates on each side) plus the weight of the machine.

Leg extension— I do this exercise last because you can easily damage you patellar tendon if you lift too much weight, which is a common mistake. Consider the angle. As you hold the weight two feet ahead of you, the 150 lbs. is intensified by the distance. Trust me when I say you are putting a tremendous amount of stress on the knee joint. Perform this exercise last when your legs are tired. I use 50 lbs. one leg at a time for almost all sets.

Leg Curls— These can be done standing on lying prone on a machine. Whichever way you choose, perform them with strict form and without momentum. I use 60, 70, 80, 90, and 100 lbs. for the prone position. Keep your hips flat against the pad and curl with your hamstrings. If you perform leg curls standing, you will use much less weight since you will only use single leg execution. Stand straight and try not to lean to the side.

Thursday—Shoulders

Dumbbell Presses— I like to sit on a Swiss Ball while performing this exercise; it requires more stabilization from the abdominal and lower back region. This results in a much stronger core. I use 50, 60, 70, and 80 lbs. This exercise is more challenging using a Swiss Ball than a traditional chair.

Lateral Raises— This exercise is often done *incorrectly* by leading with the hands, or using the "pouring from a pitcher" method. The arms should be parallel to the floor at the top of the movement. If the elbows are higher than the hands, which is often taught, the shoulder joint is put in a compromised position. I use 30, 40, 50, and 60 lbs. for this exercise.

Upright Rows, Wide Grip— I prefer to use a wide grip with this exercise to place emphasis on the medial head of the deltoid instead of the trapezius. Lead by pulling up from the elbows to a comfortable height. My weight selection is 50, 60, 70, 80, and 90 lbs. I use a barbell to perform these.

Clean & Press— I usually perform this exercise in place of upright rows. These are great for overall shoulder development and coordination. Make sure to learn the proper form before beginning. I start with a 50-lb. barbell and work my way through 60, 70, 80, 90, and 100 lbs.

Rear Delts— In addition to traditional bent raises, I like to use a rowing machine for this exercise. Many people neglect the rear deltoid muscle. Don't make the same mistake. It is important to train all muscles of the body. *Symmetry is an important element to modeling.* I use a grip that enables me to keep my elbows high. Pull with high elbows and squeeze the shoulder blades together. I start with 80, 90, 100, and 120 lbs. If I use the bent dumbbell, I use much lighter weights such as 20, 30, 40, and 50 lbs.

Friday—Arms

Close Grip Bench Press— This exercise is pretty basic. Keep the elbows tight against the body and proceed slowly. I start with 135, 155, 170, and 225 lbs.

Straight Bar Biceps Curls— I like to alternate between biceps and triceps on the same workout. I use a barbell with 50, 60, 80, 100, and 120 lbs.

Bench Dips (With Weights)— I love these! Get two benches; put your feet up on one and your hands on the other. You might need someone to put the weight on your lap. I use a dumbbell for these at 50, 60, 70, 80, 90, and 100 lbs.

Hammer Curls – This exercise works your biceps from a different angle than traditional curls do. Hammer curls target the radial brachialis muscle that leads into the forearm. Be sure that your thumb is on top. I use 30, 40, 50, and 60 lbs. for this one.

Press Downs— Keep your elbows tight against your side and avoid lifting too far past 90 degrees at the top of the movement. I use 50, 60, 70, 80, and sometimes 90 lbs.

Reverse Curls— A different angle with this exercise yields a different response. I like to use a bent bar for these with my palms facing down. I progress from 45, 55, 65, to 75 lbs.

***Reverse Press Downs*—** This exercise targets the "long head" of the triceps (the larger outer muscle that is most noticeable in a short-sleeved shirt). You will notice you won't need as much weight here. I generally use 30, 40, 50, and 60 lbs.

***Machine Curls*—** The machine curls are a terrific way to finish a great arm workout. Sit down and go for it. Keep your butt on the seat; this will ensure that you are using your biceps and not your entire body weight. I usually go light with 50, 60, 70, and 80 lbs.

In addition to the weekly workout described above, I usually alternate a calf or abdominal workout daily.

Abdominals

***Swiss Ball Crunches (With Weights)*—** You will need a Swiss ball for these. Place your feet under two dumbbells. Use twice the amount of weight than you would normally use to avoid flipping over backwards on the Swiss ball. Place a dumbbell on your chest/chin areas. While holding the dumbbell, slowly wrap your spine around the ball to stretch your abdominals. Go slow and avoid using more weight than you can handle to protect the back. Return to the sitting position while exhaling. I usually perform 10 reps with approximately a 60-lb. dumbbell.

***Ab Roller*—** No need to buy a $79 Ab Roller from an infomercial, the $10 one you used as a kid will do just fine. Be careful and only do about 5 reps per set. Keep everything tight from the shoulders down while doing this advanced exercise.

Calves

***Seated Raises (Soleus)*—** The soleus muscle responds to less sets and more reps with a lighter weight. It is comprised mainly of slow twitch fibers that respond to this stimulus. Keep this in mind when selecting your weights.

Standing Raises (Gastrocnemius)— The gastrocnemius muscle is the opposite. When training the calves while standing, remember to do more sets, fewer reps and more weight. It is a fast twitch muscle fiber.

This is a basic week for me. Remember that I do vary the workouts, but the goal I suggest to you is to master the basics first.

A Word About Nutrition

I have developed a program that works great for me. Therefore, I usually eat the same food each day to keep my body in top form. In addition, I drink at least one gallon of water each day and I take Glucosamine. My supplemation is very limited. I use only meal replacements, multi-vitamins, and EFAs. On occasion, I will use creatine.

A typical day:

Meal One— A handful of oatmeal with one scoop of protein powder, multi-vitamins (with EFAs).

Meal Two— Canned chicken breast mixed with one tablespoon of safflower mayonnaise and one can of green beans.

Meal Three— Meal replacement powder.

Meal Four— Three-fourths of a pound of lean ground turkey patties with a medium-sized yam.

Meal Five— Canned chicken breast with one tablespoon safflower mayonnaise and one can of green beans.

Meal Six— Fresh Albacore tuna, broccoli, half cup of rice, and a second pack of multi-vitamins (with EFAs).

There you have it. This is my program—basic, but effective.

A Few Words of Thanks.

As I look back over the years of my career in the fitness world, I have realized that I have been very fortunate to reach the levels of success that I have. I have worked very hard, made good and bad decisions, but for the most part, the entire experience has been very enjoyable.

I do know one thing, I would be very wrong if I didn't acknowledge some people who have been instrumental in helping me get where I am today. Most books have an acknowledgement paragraph at the beginning. I feel that it deserves an entire chapter for this book.

Often time, when someone attempts to give recognition to people, they run the risk of hurt feelings or forgotten heroes. I want to clarify that I am mentioning people who were directly related to my success in this industry. If I were writing another book, there would be other names mentioned based on the subject matter. I hope this helps!

Where do I begin? At the beginning I guess. I realize that genetics had much to do with my physique, so I must give props to my Mom and Dad. I am not as tall as I would like to be, but I guess I can forgive you for that little flaw.

I remember my very first official shoot; it was for a poster and eventually my first cover. It was the *Penny Saver*, but it was a cover. Noel Grady has been a friend and supporter of mine for years and he is officially the first one to shoot me in a professional environment. Thanks Noel.

I realized early on that competitive bodybuilding would be the place to be seen, so I began to enter contests. I did local, small shows to no avail, but then I did *Muscle Mania* and the rest is history. Lou Zwick promotes the best shows for the athletes and media. This is where I was discovered. Lou, thank you for being my friend and pumping me up.

After my first *Muscle Mania* competition, I was approached by an associate of Martin Ryter. He asked if I was interested in doing a photo shoot and I quickly accepted the offer. Soon I found myself in front of Martin's camera, which shortly turned into my first cover of a real magazine. Martin has been a great friend, a source of reliable information, and a constant supporter ever since. Thanks, Martin!

If you read the forward of the book, you know how I met Ralph Dehaan. Ralph is a very good friend and our relationship has blossomed since that initial meeting. In addition to calling me for shoots, he has taught me some of the finer points of working on the other side of the lens. I have set lights, changed film, learned exposures and other elements of what he does. This has made me better at what I do. Ralph, lets keep working bro. You are a good man, thank you for everything.

At my next *Muscle Mania* competition, I met some very key people. A man with a very peculiar accent approached me. He was polite, well-spoken and a big fan of the sport. As we talked, I found him to be willing and able to help me meet the right people that could assist me to further my career. Howard Flaks has continually done that for me over the years since that contest. Every time he sees an opportunity he feels I can benefit from, he calls to inform me of it. He also introduced me to Kal Yee at that show. Howard had the remedy for both needs, Kal needed someone to shoot for the cover of *Muscle & Fitness* and I wanted to be the guy. Howard made the introduction and the rest is history. My first *M & F* cover came as a result of that encounter in the hallway at the show. Howard, thank you for always encouraging me.

I'm going to have to shorten these thank you's, or I'll be here forever! I think the rest of you will understand. I love ya just the same.

Jason Ellis, thank you for inspiring me to write this book. Our brainstorming sessions are paying off, my friend. Rick Schaff, man I am so happy we met. You have been a tremendous help. Sherry and Frank Giardina, you guys played a big part, thank you! Bill Lykins, the producer of my show, thanks for providing a venue to help me be seen. Nick Kellis, you make me sound good when I talk. Many thanks to Bill Phillips and the crew at *Muscle Media*—Kal,

Todd, Elaine, and both Jeff's. All the people at *Muscle & Fitness*. Joe and Sean and everyone at *Max Muscle*. Everyone at *FitnessAge*. Monica Brant, Alex Ardenti, and James DeMelo, my friend and mentor who keeps me focused on God in my life. You have been there for me in the important times, thank you! Rocco, Jason, and Michelle, I love you guys. Rich King, my lifelong friend, thanks for listening and encouraging me during the hard times.

Now I think I know why everyone else does a short paragraph at the beginning of the book. I could go on forever!

I would be remised if I didn't give the biggest thanks of all to my wife Anita. Man, I gotta tell all of you. She is awesome. Think about it, she has put up with me all of these years—traveling, working with models, and not making any money for the longest time. I don't need to go on. Anita, thank you. I love and appreciate you more than you know. Has it paid off? Was it worth it? I hope so. Taylor and Mitchell, I love you kids. You are the best!

Again, a huge thanks to each and every one of you and anyone I may have forgotten. I hope in some way I have been a blessing in your life, because all of you have been in mine. I pray that God will bless each one of you with the desires of your heart. I wish all the best to you in your careers and all that you do in your lifetime.